100 Days of Character

Daily Devotional

STEPHEN ARTERBURN

100 DAYS OF CHARACTER

Aspire Press is an imprint of
Rose Publishing, LLC
140 Summit Street
P. O. Box 3473
Peabody, Massachusetts 01961-3473
www.hendricksonrose.com

Book cover and layout design by Sergio Urquiza

ISBN: 9781628624953

Printed through Asia Pacific Offset Ltd
Printed in China
April 2018, 1st Printing

This book is given to

____

on this day

____

Contents

Introduction

Sometimes it seems that life in the twenty-first century has been designed with an overriding purpose in mind: to test—and if possible, to tear down—your character. At almost every turn, you are tempted to take shortcuts, to follow the wrong role models, and to betray your conscience. If you fall prey to these temptations, you will inevitably disappoint your family, your community, and yourself. A far better strategy, of course, is to guard your integrity like you guard your wallet, and this book is intended to help.

This text contains one hundred devotional readings that are intended to remind you of the importance of character: keeping it, building it, and passing it on to the next generation.

This text contains biblically based prescriptions for the inevitable challenges that accompany life here on Earth. As you consider your own circumstances, remember this: whatever the size of your challenge, whatever the scope of your temptation or your problem, God is bigger. Much bigger. He will instruct you, protect you, energize you, and heal you if you let him. So let him. Pray fervently, listen carefully, work diligently, and treat every single day as an exercise in character building, because that's precisely what every day can be . . . and should be.

> *Blessed is the one who does not walk in step with the wicked or stand in the way that sinners take or sit in the company of mockers, but whose delight is in the law of the Lord, and who meditates on his law day and night. That person is like a tree planted by streams of water, which yields its fruit in season and whose leaf does not wither—whatever they do prospers* (Psalm 1:1–3).

During the next one hundred days, you will be challenged to examine your habits, your thoughts, your priorities, and your behaviors. And you'll be challenged to consider proven formulas for character building—strategies for making the most of the talents and the opportunities that have been given to you by your Creator.

Building Character through Honesty

The Lord detests lying lips, but he delights in people who are trustworthy.

Proverbs 12:22

As Christians, we are called to walk with God and to obey his commandments. But we live in a world that presents us with countless temptations to wander far from God's path. These temptations have the potential to destroy us, in part, because they cause us to be dishonest with ourselves and with others.

Dishonesty is a habit. Once we start bending the truth, we're likely to keep bending it. Honesty, like its counterpart, is also a habit, a habit that pays powerful dividends for those who place character above convenience.

So, for the next ninety-nine days, make this simple promise to yourself and keep it: when you're tempted to bend the truth, even slightly—or to break it—ask yourself this question: "What does God want me to do?" Then listen carefully to your conscience. When you do, your actions will be honorable, and your character will take care of itself.

Take time to think about your own character, both your strong points and your weaknesses. Then list three aspects of your character—long-standing habits or troublesome behaviors—that you would like to modify during the next ninety-nine days. Finally, ask God to be your partner as you take steps to improve yourself and your life.

Character cannot be developed in ease and quiet. Only through experience of trial and suffering can the soul be strengthened, vision cleared, ambition inspired, and success achieved.

HELEN KELLER

No man can use his Bible with power unless he has the character of Jesus in his heart.

ALAN REDPATH

Right actions done for the wrong reason do not help to build the internal quality of character called a "virtue," and it is this quality or character that really matters.

C. S. LEWIS

For Further Reflection

Proverbs 10:9; 20:7; Romans 5:3–4; 1 Timothy 2:2, 7

Today's Prayer

Dear Lord, every day can be an exercise in character building, and that's what I intend to make this day. I will be mindful that my thoughts and actions have great consequences, both in my own life and in the lives of my loved ones. I will strive to make my thoughts and actions pleasing to you so that I may be an instrument of your peace today and every day. Amen.

Building Character by Putting God First

Seek first his kingdom and his righteousness, and all these things will be given to you as well.

Matthew 6:33

One of the quickest ways to build character—perhaps the only way—is to do it with God as your partner. So here are a couple of questions worth thinking about:

- Have you made God your top priority by offering him your heart, your soul, your talents, and your time?
- Or are you in the habit of giving God little more than a few hours on Sunday morning?

The answers to these questions will determine, to a surprising extent, the direction of your day and the condition of your character.

As you contemplate your own relationship with God, remember this: all of humankind is engaged in the practice of worship. Some folks choose to worship God and, as a result, reap the joy that he intends for his children to experience. Other folks—folks who are stubbornly determined to do it "their way"—distance themselves from God by worshiping such things as earthly possessions or personal gratification . . . and when they do, they suffer.

Think about your priorities. Are you really putting God first in your life, or are you putting other things—like possessions, pleasures, or personal status—ahead of your relationship with the Father? And if your priorities for life are misaligned, think of at least three things you can do today to put God where he belongs: in first place.

We become whatever we are committed to.

RICK WARREN

God calls us to be committed to Him, to be committed to making a difference, and to be committed to reconciliation.

BILL HYBELS

One with God is a majority.

BILLY GRAHAM

For Further Reflection

Exodus 20:3; Deuteronomy 6:4–5;
Isaiah 64:8; 1 John 4:8, 12–13

Today's Prayer

Dear Lord, today I will honor you with my thoughts, my actions, and my prayers. I will seek to please you, and I will strive to serve you. Your blessings are as limitless as your love. And because I have been so richly blessed, I will worship you, Father, with thanksgiving in my heart and praise on my lips this day and forever. Amen.

The Right Kind of Example?

Don't let anyone look down on you because you are young, but set an example for the believers in speech, in conduct, in love, in faith and in purity.

1 Timothy 4:12

Whether you know it or not, you're a role model. Your friends and family members watch your actions and make careful mental notes about what those actions reveal about your character.

- What kind of example are you?
- Are you the kind of person whose life serves as a model of integrity and righteousness?
- Are you a believer whose behavior serves as a positive role model for others?
- Are you the kind of Christian whose actions, day in and day out, are based upon kindness, faithfulness, and a love for the Lord?

If so, you are not only blessed by God, but you are also a powerful force for good in a world that desperately needs positive influences such as yours.

Corrie ten Boom advised, "Don't worry about what you do not understand. Worry about what you do understand in the Bible but do not live by." That's sound advice because your family and friends are watching . . . and so, for that matter, is God.

Your life is a sermon. What kind of sermon will you preach? The words you choose to speak may have some impact on others but not nearly as much impact as the life you choose to live. Today, pause to consider the tone, the theme, and the context of your particular sermon, and ask yourself if it's a message that you're proud to deliver.

In your desire to share the gospel, you may be the only Jesus someone else will ever meet. Be real and be involved with people.

BARBARA JOHNSON

Living life with a consistent spiritual walk deeply influences those we love most.

VONETTE BRIGHT

In our faith we follow in someone's steps. In our faith we leave footprints to guide others. It's the principle of discipleship.

MAX LUCADO

For Further Reflection

Matthew 5:14, 16; Philippians 2:14–15;
Titus 2:7; Hebrews 12:1; James 3:13

Today's Prayer

Lord, make me a worthy example to my family and friends. And let my words and my deeds serve as a testimony to the changes you have made in my life. Let me praise you, Father, by following in the footsteps of your Son, and let others see him through me. Amen.

Faith Builds Character

Truly I tell you, if anyone says to this mountain, "Go, throw yourself into the sea," and does not doubt in their heart but believes that what they say will happen, it will be done for them.

MARK 11:23

Because we live in a demanding world, all of us have mountains to climb and mountains to move. Moving those mountains requires faith. And the experience of trying, with God's help, to move mountains builds character.

- Are you a mountain-moving person whose faith is evident for all to see?
- Or are you a spiritual underachiever?

As you think about the answer to those questions, consider this: God needs more people who are willing to move mountains for his glory and for his kingdom.

Every life–including yours–is a series of wins and losses. Every step of the way, through every triumph and tragedy, God walks with you, ready and willing to strengthen you. So the next time you find your character being tested, remember to take your fears to God. If you call upon him, you will be comforted. Whatever your challenge, whatever your trouble, God can handle it.

So strengthen your faith through praise, through worship, through Bible study, and through prayer. And trust God's plans. With him, all things are possible, and he stands ready to open a world of possibilities to you . . . if you have faith.

Today, think about the times you've been hesitant to share your faith. And as you contemplate the day ahead, think about three specific ways that you can vocalize your faith to family and friends.

I do not want merely to possess a faith; I want a faith that possesses me.

CHARLES KINGSLEY

Only God can move mountains, but faith and prayer can move God.

E. M. BOUNDS

How do you walk in faith? By claiming the promises of God and obeying the Word of God, in spite of what you see, how you feel, or what may happen.

WARREN WIERSBE

FOR FURTHER REFLECTION

2 Chronicles 20:20; Mark 9:23; 1 Timothy 6:12; Hebrews 11:6; 1 John 5:4

Today's Prayer

Dear Lord, I want faith that moves mountains. You have big plans for this world and big plans for me. Help me fulfill those plans, Father, as I follow in the footsteps of your Son. Amen.

A World Brimming with Temptation

No temptation has overtaken you except what is common to mankind. And God is faithful; he will not let you be tempted beyond what you can bear. But when you are tempted, he will also provide a way out so that you can endure it.

1 Corinthians 10:13

It's inevitable: today you will be tempted by somebody or something–in fact, you will probably be tempted on countless occasions. Here's the good news: the Creator has promised that with his help, you can resist every single temptation that confronts you.

God is always with you, and if you do your part, he will do his part. But what, precisely, is your part? A good starting point is simply learning how to recognize the subtle temptations that surround you. The images of immorality are ubiquitous, and they're intended to hijack your mind, your heart, your pocketbook, your life, and your soul. Don't let them do it.

Satan is both industrious and creative; he's working 24/7, and he's causing pain, heartache, trauma, and tragedy in more ways than ever before. You, as a Christian, must remain watchful and strong–starting today and ending never.

Ask yourself these important questions:

- "What images, people, or places am I likely to encounter today that might encourage me to think impure thoughts?"

- "How will I prepare myself to respond to these temptations?"

Most Christians do not know or fully realize that the adversary of our lives is Satan and that his main tool is our flesh, our old nature.

Bill Bright

Many jokes are made about the devil, but the devil is no joke. He is called a deceiver. In order to accomplish his purpose, the devil blinds people to their need for Christ. Two forces are at work in our world–the forces of Christ and the forces of the devil–and you are asked to choose.

Billy Graham

A man who gives in to temptation after five minutes simply does not know what it would have been like an hour later.

C. S. Lewis

For Further Reflection

Ephesians 6:11; Hebrews 4:15-16;
James 1:12; 1 Peter 5:8-9; 2 Peter 2:9

Today's Prayer

Lord, life is filled with temptations to stray from your chosen path. But I face no temptation that you have not already met and conquered through my Lord and Savior Jesus Christ, the One who empowers me with his strength and his love.
Amen.

Discipline Builds Character

I strike a blow to my body and make it my slave so that after I have preached to others, I myself will not be disqualified for the prize.

1 Corinthians 9:27

God's Word reminds us again and again that our Creator expects us to lead disciplined lives. God doesn't reward laziness, misbehavior, or apathy. To the contrary, he expects us to behave with dignity and discipline. Unfortunately, we live in a world in which leisure is glorified and indifference is often glamorized. But God gives us talents, and he expects us to use them.

Proverbs 23:12 advises: "Listen to advice and accept discipline, and at the end you will be counted among the wise." And 2 Peter 1:5–6 teaches, "Make every effort to add to your faith goodness; and to goodness, knowledge; and to knowledge, self-control; and to self-control, perseverance; and to perseverance, godliness." Thus, God's Word is clear: we must exercise self-discipline in all matters.

If we genuinely seek to be faithful stewards of our time, our talents, and our resources, we must adopt a disciplined approach to life. Otherwise, our talents are wasted and our resources are squandered. Life's greatest rewards seldom fall into our laps; to the contrary, our greatest accomplishments usually require work, perseverance, and discipline.

A disciplined lifestyle gives you more control: The more disciplined you become, the more you can take control over your life (which, by the way, is far better than letting your life take control over you).

Personal humility is a spiritual discipline and the hallmark of the service of Jesus.

FRANKLIN GRAHAM

Simply stated, self-discipline is obedience to God's Word and willingness to submit everything in life to His will, for His ultimate glory.

JOHN MACARTHUR

A spiritual discipline is necessary in order to move slowly from an absurd to an obedient life, from a life filled with noisy worries to a life in which there is some free inner space where we can listen to our God and follow his guidance.

HENRI NOUWEN

For Further Reflection

Proverbs 9:13; 10:17; 16:20; Hebrews 12:5, 11

Today's Prayer

Lord, I want to be a disciplined believer. Let me use my time wisely, and let me teach others by the faithfulness of my conduct today and every day. Amen.

Choices That Build Character

This day I call the heavens and the earth as witnesses against you that I have set before you life and death, blessings and curses. Now choose life, so that you and your children may live and that you may love the Lord your God, listen to his voice, and hold fast to him.

DEUTERONOMY 30:19–20

Life is a series of choices. From the instant we wake in the morning until the moment we nod off to sleep at night, we make countless decisions:

- About the things we do
- About the words we speak
- About the thoughts we choose to think

Simply put, the quality of those decisions determines the quality of our lives.

Sometimes, because you're an imperfect human being, you may become so wrapped up in meeting society's expectations that you fail to focus on God's expectations. Instead, seek God's guidance as you focus your energies on becoming the best "you" that you can be.

Take time to consider how many things in this life you can control: your thoughts, your words, your priorities, and your actions, for starters. And then, if you sincerely want to discover God's purpose for your life, make choices that are pleasing to him. He deserves no less . . . and neither do you.

If you'd like to strengthen your character by making good choices, try spending more time really getting to know God. How? Through worship, praise, Bible study, prayer, and silent meditation. Make the choice to know God better today and every day.

Life is a series of choices between the bad, the good, and the best. Everything depends on how we choose.

VANCE HAVNER

Every day, I find countless opportunities to decide whether I will obey God and demonstrate my love for Him or try to please myself or the world system. God is waiting for my choices.

BILL BRIGHT

We are either the masters or the victims of our attitudes. It is a matter of personal choice. Who we are today is the result of choices we made yesterday. Tomorrow, we will become what we choose today. To change means to choose to change.

JOHN MAXWELL

For Further Reflection

Proverbs 3:1–35; 16:9; Matthew 6:33; 7:13–14; Galatians 6:7–8

Today's Prayer

Heavenly Father, I have many choices to make. Help me choose wisely as I follow in the footsteps of your only begotten Son. Amen.

Studying God's Word Builds Character

You will be a good minister of Christ Jesus, nourished on the truths of the faith and of the good teaching that you have followed.

1 Timothy 4:6

God's promises are found in the Holy Bible—a road map for life here on Earth and for life eternal. As Christians, we are called to trust its promises, to follow its commandments, and to share its Good News.

The Bible records the promises God has made to humankind and that includes you. God's promises never fail and they never grow old.

- Are you standing on the promises of God?
- Are you expecting God to do wonderful things?
- Or are you living beneath a cloud of apprehension and doubt?

For passionate believers, every day begins and ends with God's Son and God's promises. When we accept Christ into our hearts, God promises us the opportunity for earthly peace and spiritual abundance. But more importantly, God promises us the priceless gift of eternal life.

As we face the inevitable challenges of life here on Earth, we must arm ourselves with the promises of God's Holy Word. When we do, we can expect the best, not only for the day ahead, but also for all eternity.

Trust God's Word. Charles Swindoll writes, "There are four words I wish we would never forget, and they are, 'God keeps his word.'"

God gives us a compass and a Book of promises and principles–the Bible–and lets us make our decisions day by day as we sense the leading of His Spirit. This is how we grow.

Warren Wiersbe

The Reference Point for the Christian is the Bible. All values, judgments, and attitudes must be gauged in relationship to this Reference Point.

Ruth Bell Graham

Study the Bible and observe how the persons behaved and how God dealt with them. There is explicit teaching on every condition of life.

Corrie ten Boom

For Further Reflection

Matthew 24:35; John 8:47; 2 Timothy 3:16-17; Hebrews 4:12; 1 Peter 1:25

Today's Prayer

Heavenly Father, your Word is a light unto the world; I will study it and trust it, and share it. In all that I do, help me be a worthy witness for you as I share the Good News of your perfect Son and your perfect Word. Amen.

Optimism Builds Character

I can do all this through him who gives me strength.

Philippians 4:13

As each day unfolds, you are quite literally surrounded by more opportunities than you can count—opportunities to improve your own life and the lives of those you love. God's Word promises that you, like all of God's children, possess the ability to experience earthly peace and spiritual abundance. Yet sometimes—especially if you dwell upon the inevitable disappointments that may, at times, befall even the luckiest among us—you may allow pessimism to invade your thoughts and your heart.

It's undeniable: the self-fulfilling prophecy is alive, well, and living at your house. If you constantly anticipate the worst, that's what you're likely to attract. But if you make the effort to think positive thoughts, you'll increase the probability that those positive thoughts will come true.

So here's a simple, character-building tip for improving your life: put the self-fulfilling prophecy to work for you. Expect the best, and then get busy working to achieve it. When you do, you'll not only increase the odds of achieving your dreams, but you'll also have more fun along the way.

Be a realistic optimist. Your attitude will help create your future. So think realistically about yourself and your situation while making a conscious effort to focus on hopes, not fears. When you do, you'll put the self-fulfilling prophecy to work for you.

It is a remarkable thing that some of the most optimistic and enthusiastic people you will meet are those who have been through intense suffering.

Warren Wiersbe

The Christian lifestyle is not one of legalistic do's and don'ts, but one that is positive, attractive, and joyful.

Vonette Bright

Christ can put a spring in your step and a thrill in your heart. Optimism and cheerfulness are products of knowing Christ.

Billy Graham

For Further Reflection

Psalms 23:5-6; 27:1; 51:8; Romans 8:25; 2 Timothy 1:7

Today's Prayer

Lord, you care for me, you love me, and you have given me the priceless gift of eternal life through your Son, Jesus. Because of you, Lord, I have every reason to live each day with celebration and hope. Help me to face this day with a spirit of optimism and thanksgiving so that I may lift the spirits of those I meet as I share the Good News of your Son. Amen.

Adversity Builds Character

God is our refuge and strength, an ever-present help in trouble. Therefore we will not fear, though the earth give way and the mountains fall into the heart of the sea.

Psalm 46:1–2

It's inevitable. We will encounter disappointments and setbacks in our lives. But even on our darkest days, we must remember that God's love remains constant. And we must never forget that God intends for us to use our setbacks as stepping stones on the path to a better life.

The fact that we encounter adversity is not nearly so important as the way we choose to deal with it. When tough times arrive, we have a clear choice: we can begin the difficult work of tackling our troubles . . . or not. If we refuse to address our problems, even a small annoyance can grow into a king-sized catastrophe.

The words of Jesus offer us comfort: "I have told you these things, so that in me you may have peace. In this world you will have trouble. But take heart! I have overcome the world" (John 16:33).

As believers, we know:

- God loves us and that he will protect us.
- In times of hardship, he will comfort us.
- In times of sorrow, he will dry our tears.

- When we are troubled, weak, or sorrowful, God is always with us.

If you're having tough times, talking things over with someone you can really trust is usually helpful. So if your troubles seem overwhelming, be willing to seek outside help. Ask God to guide you to the right person.

Your greatest ministry will likely come out of your greatest hurt.

Rick Warren

God will not permit any troubles to come upon us unless He has a specific plan by which great blessing can come out of the difficulty.

Peter Marshall

Jesus does not say, "There is no storm." He says, "I am here, do not toss, but trust."

Vance Havner

For Further Reflection

Psalms 9:9; 56:13; Matthew 11:28–30;
Romans 5:3–4; Philippians 4:6–7

Today's Prayer

Heavenly Father, you are my strength and my refuge. As I journey through this day, I know that I may encounter disappointments and losses. When I am troubled, let me turn to you. Keep me steady, Lord, and renew a right spirit inside of me this day and forever. Amen.

Prayer Builds Character

If you believe, you will receive
whatever you ask for in prayer.

MATTHEW 21:22

God promises that the prayers of righteous men and women can accomplish great things. God promises that he answers prayer (although his answers are not always in accordance with our desires). God invites us to be still and to feel his presence. So pray. Start praying before the sun comes up and keep praying until you fall off to sleep at night. Pray about matters great and small, and be watchful for the answers that God most assuredly sends your way.

- Is prayer an integral part of your daily life or is it a hit-or-miss routine?
- Do you "pray continually" (1 Thessalonians 5:17), or is your prayer life an afterthought?
- Do you regularly pray in solitude, or do you bow your head only when others are watching?

Prayer strengthens your character and your relationship with God . . . so pray. Martin Luther observed, "If I should neglect prayer but a single day, I should lose a great deal of the fire of faith." Those words apply to you, too. And it's up to you to live—and to pray—accordingly.

The quality of your spiritual life will be in direct proportion to the quality of your prayer life. Prayer changes things, and it changes you. Instead of worrying about your next decision, ask God to lead the way. Don't limit your prayers to meals or to bedtime; pray constantly. God is listening, he wants to hear from you, and you most certainly need to hear from him. Today, instead of turning things over in your mind, turn them over to God in prayer.

When there is a matter that requires definite prayer, pray until you believe God and until you can thank Him for His answer.

Hannah Whitall Smith

Prayer connects us with God's limitless potential.

Henry Blackaby

God shapes the world by prayer. The more praying there is in the world, the better the world will be, and the mightier will be the forces against evil.

E. M. Bounds

For Further Reflection

Psalm 19:14; Luke 5:16; Romans 12:12; Philippians 4:6; James 5:16

Today's Prayer

Dear Lord, I will open my heart to you. I will take my concerns, my fears, my plans, and my hopes to you in prayer. And, then, I will trust the answers that you give. You are my loving Father, and I will accept your will for my life today and every day.

Amen.

Forgiveness Now

Peter came to Jesus and asked, "Lord, how many times shall I forgive my brother or sister who sins against me? Up to seven times?" Jesus answered, "I tell you, not seven times, but seventy-seven times."

MATTHEW 18:21–22

When we have been injured or embarrassed, we feel the urge to strike back and to hurt the ones who have hurt us. But Christ instructs us to do otherwise: "Love your enemies and pray for those who persecute you" (Matthew 5:44). Christ teaches us that forgiveness is God's way.

- Do you invest more time reliving the past than you should?
- Are you troubled by feelings of anger, bitterness, envy, or regret?
- Do you harbor ill will against someone whom you simply can't seem to forgive?

If you answered yes to one or more of these questions, it's time to get serious about forgiveness.

Most of us don't spend too much time thinking about forgiveness; we worry, instead, about the injustices we have suffered and the people who inflicted them. God has a better plan: he wants us to live in the present, not the past, and he knows that in order to do so, we must forgive those who have harmed us.

Today, make a list of the people you need to forgive. Then make up your mind to forgive at least one person on that list. Finally, ask God to cleanse your heart of bitterness, animosity, and regret. If you ask him sincerely and often, he will respond.

God expects us to forgive others as He has forgiven us; we are to follow His example by having a forgiving heart.

Vonette Bright

Learning how to forgive and forget is one of the secrets of a happy Christian life.

Warren Wiersbe

Forgiveness is actually the best revenge because it not only sets us free from the person we forgive, but it frees us to move into all that God has in store for us.

Stormie Omartian

For Further Reflection

Mark 11:25; Luke 6:36-37; 11:4;
Ephesians 4:32; Colossians 3:13-14

Today's Prayer

Lord, I know that I need to forgive others just as you have forgiven me. Keep me mindful, Father, that I am never fully liberated until I have been freed from the chains of bitterness—and that you offer me that freedom through your Son, Christ Jesus. Amen.

The Need to Lead

In the Lord's hand the king's heart is a stream of water that he channels toward all who please him.

Proverbs 21:1

If you are in a position of leadership—whether at church, home, work, or school—it's up to you to set the right tone by making hard decisions and by setting a proper example. But make no mistake: wise leaders don't take things too seriously. The best leaders learn:

- When to laugh (when it's appropriate)
- When to have fun (the good, clean kind)
- When to lead (by example, of course)

Are you the kind of leader whom you would want to follow? If so, congratulations. But if the answer to that question is in question, it's time to improve your leadership skills, beginning with the words that you speak and the example that you set.

If you occupy a position of leadership, then you should prepare yourself for the time when you will be faced with a tough, unpopular decision. When that day arrives, you have a choice to make: you can either do the right thing or do the easy thing. Do the right thing.

Today, think about your own leadership style. Remember that leadership comes in many forms and that you will probably be more effective using your own style, not by trying to copy someone else's. When it comes to leadership, an original version of yourself is far better than a weak imitation of someone else.

The test of a leader is taking the vision from me to we.

John Maxwell

A wise leader chooses a variety of gifted individuals. He complements his strengths.

Charles Stanley

People who inspire others are those who see invisible bridges at the end of dead-end streets.

Charles Swindoll

For Further Reflection

Matthew 25:21; Romans 12:6–8;
1 Thessalonians 5:14; 1 Timothy 3:2–3; 1 Peter 5:2

Today's Prayer

Dear Lord, when I find myself in a position of leadership, let me seek your will and obey your commandments. Make me a person of integrity and wisdom, Lord, and make me a worthy example to my family, friends, and coworkers. Let me be a Christ-centered leader; and let me turn to you, Father, for guidance, for courage, for wisdom, and for love. Amen.

What Is Your Focus?

Let your eyes look straight ahead; fix your gaze directly before you. Give careful thought to the paths for your feet and be steadfast in all your ways. Do not turn to the right or the left; keep your foot from evil.

Proverbs 4:25–27

The condition of your character is determined, to a surprising extent, by the direction of your thoughts. If you focus your thoughts and energies on matters that honor your God, your family, and yourself, you will reap rich rewards. But if you focus too intently on the distractions and temptations of the world, you're inviting large quantities of trouble.

- What is your focus today?
- Are you willing to focus your thoughts and energies on God's blessings and upon his will for your life?
- Or will you turn your thoughts to other things?

Consider this: God created you in his own image, and he wants you to experience joy and abundance. But God will not force his joy upon you; you must claim it for yourself.

A person who dabbles in the Christian faith is unwilling to place God above all other things. Resist that temptation; make God the cornerstone and the touchstone of your life. When you do, he will give you all the strength and wisdom you need to live victoriously for him.

Ask yourself if you're truly focusing your thoughts and energies on matters that are pleasing to God and beneficial to your family. Then ask your Creator to help you focus on his love, his Son, and his plan for your life.

Only the man who follows the command of Jesus single-mindedly and unresistingly let his yoke rest upon him, finds his burden easy, and under its gentle pressure receives the power to persevere in the right way.

DIETRICH BONHOEFFER

Give me the person who says, "This one thing I do, and not these fifty things I dabble in."

D. L. MOODY

Paul did one thing. Most of us dabble in forty things. Are you a doer or a dabbler?

VANCE HAVNER

For Further Reflection

Matthew 6:34; 7:13–14; Philippians 3:15–16; Hebrews 12:1–2

Today's Prayer

Dear Lord, help me to face this day with a spirit of optimism and thanksgiving. And let me focus my thoughts on you and your incomparable gifts. Amen.

Living on Purpose

For in him all things were created: things in heaven and on earth, visible and invisible, whether thrones or powers or rulers or authorities; all things have been created through him and for him.

Colossians 1:16

God has a plan for the universe, and he has a plan for you. He understands that plan as thoroughly and completely as he knows you. If you seek God's will earnestly and prayerfully, he will make his plans known to you in his own time and in his own way.

Do you sincerely seek to discover God's purpose for your life? If so, you must first be willing to live in accordance with his commandments. You must also study God's Word and be watchful for his signs. Finally, you should open yourself up to the Creator every day–beginning with this one–and you must have faith that he will soon reveal his plans to you.

Sometimes, God's plans and purposes may seem unmistakably clear to you. If so, push ahead. But other times, he may lead you through the wilderness before he directs you to the promised land. So be patient and keep seeking his will for your life. When you do, you'll be amazed at the marvelous things that an all-powerful, all-knowing God can do.

Perhaps you're in a hurry to understand God's unfolding plan for your life. If so, remember that God operates according to a perfect timetable–his, not yours. So be patient. God has big things in store for you, but he may have quite a few lessons to teach you before you are fully prepared to do his will and fulfill his purpose.

When God speaks to you through the Bible, prayer, circumstances, the church, or in some other way, He has a purpose in mind for your life.

HENRY BLACKABY AND CLAUDE KING

The greatest tragedy is not death, but life without purpose.

RICK WARREN

Let us live with urgency. Let us exploit the opportunity of life. Let us not drift. Let us live intentionally. We must not trifle our lives away.

RAYMOND ORTLUND

For Further Reflection

Psalms 16:11; 32:8; Proverbs 16:3; Romans 8:28; Philippians 2:13

Today's Prayer

Dear Lord, let your purposes be my purposes. Let your priorities be my priorities. Let your will be my will. Let your Word be my guide. And let me grow in faith and in wisdom today and every day. Amen.

Beyond Fear

I sought the Lord, and he answered me;
he delivered me from all my fears.

Psalm 34:4

During the darker days of life, we are wise to remember the words of Jesus, who reassured his disciples, saying, "Take courage! It is I. Don't be afraid" (Matthew 14:27).

- We live in a world that can be, at times, a very frightening place.
- We live in a world that is, at times, a very discouraging place.
- We live in a world where life-changing losses can be so painful and so profound that it seems we will never recover.

But with God's help and with the help of encouraging family members and friends, we can recover.

Are you willing to face your fears right now? Are you willing to cast off the chains of timidity and procrastination by deciding to do what needs to be done now, not later? If the answer to these questions is yes, then you're destined to build a better life for yourself and your loved ones.

Are you feeling anxious or fearful? If so, trust God to handle those problems that are simply too big for you to solve. Entrust the future—your future—to God. Then, spend a few minutes thinking about specific steps you can take to confront—and conquer—your fears.

Fear and doubt are conquered by a faith that rejoices. And faith can rejoice because the promises of God are as certain as God Himself.

KAY ARTHUR

When once we are assured that God is good, then there can be nothing left to fear.

HANNAH WHITALL SMITH

One of the main missions of God is to free us from the debilitating bonds of fear and anxiety. God's heart is broken when He sees us so demoralized and weighed down by fear.

BILL HYBELS

For Further Reflection

Psalm 23:4; Isaiah 12:2; 41:10, 13; Mark 5:36

Today's Prayer

Your Word reminds me, Lord, that even when I walk through the valley of the shadow of death, I need fear no evil, for you are with me, and you comfort me. Thank you, Lord, for a perfect love that casts out fear. Let me live courageously and faithfully this day and every day. Amen.

Sharing Your Faith Builds Character

In your hearts revere Christ as Lord. Always be prepared to give an answer to everyone who asks you to give the reason for the hope that you have.

1 Peter 3:15

Have you made the decision to allow Christ to reign over your heart? If so, you have an important story to tell: yours.

Your personal testimony is profoundly important, but perhaps because of shyness (or because of the fear of being rebuffed), you've been hesitant to share your experiences. If so, you should start paying less attention to your own insecurities and more attention to the message that God wants you to share with the world.

In his second letter to Timothy, Paul shares a message to believers of every generation when he writes, "The Spirit God gave us does not make us timid" (1:7). Paul's meaning is clear: when sharing our testimonies, we must be courageous, forthright, and unashamed.

When we let other people know the details of our faith, we assume an important responsibility–the responsibility of making certain that our words are reinforced by our actions. When we share our testimonies, we must also be willing to serve as shining examples of righteousness–undeniable examples of the changes that Jesus makes in the lives of those who accept him as their Savior.

Are you willing to follow in the footsteps of Jesus? If so, you must also be willing to talk about him. And make no mistake—the time to express your belief in him is now. You know how he has touched your own heart; help him do the same for others.

Claim the joy that is yours. Pray. And know that your joy is used by God to reach others.

Kay Arthur

There is nothing anybody else can do that can stop God from using us. We can turn everything into a testimony.

Corrie ten Boom

The sermon of your life in tough times ministers to people more powerfully than the most eloquent speaker.

Bill Bright

For Further Reflection

Matthew 5:14-16; 10:27; Luke 12:8-9;
Acts 23:11; Galatians 6:14

Today's Prayer

Lord, the life that I live and the words that I speak will tell my family and the world how I feel about you. Today and every day, let my testimony be worthy of you. Let my words be sure and true, and let my actions point others to you. Amen.

Character and Maturity

Do not conform to the pattern of this world, but be transformed by the renewing of your mind. Then you will be able to test and approve what God's will is—his good, pleasing and perfect will.

Romans 12:2

Character building never happens overnight. To the contrary, the journey toward spiritual maturity lasts a lifetime. As Christians, we can and should continue to grow in the love and the knowledge of our Savior as long as we live.

When we cease to grow, either emotionally or spiritually, we do ourselves a profound disservice. But we will not be stagnant believers if we:

- Study God's Word
- Obey his commandments
- Live in the center of his will

Instead, we will be growing Christians. And that's exactly what God intends for us to be.

When we choose to honor the Creator with our thoughts, our prayers, and our actions, we keep growing day by day . . . and that's precisely what each of us should do.

Today, think about the quality of the choices that you've made recently. Are these choices helping you become a more mature Christian? If so, don't change. If not, think about the quality of your decisions, the consequences of those decisions, and the steps that you can take to make better decisions.

As I have continued to grow in my Christian maturity, I have discovered that the Holy Spirit does not let me get by with anything.

Anne Graham Lotz

God's plan for our guidance is for us to grow gradually in wisdom before we get to the cross roads.

Bill Hybels

Being a Christian means accepting the terms of creation, accepting God as our maker and redeemer, and growing day by day into an increasingly glorious creature in Christ, developing joy, experiencing love, maturing in peace.

Eugene Peterson

For Further Reflection

1 Corinthians 13:11; Philippians 1:6; Hebrews 6:1; James 1:2–4; 2 Peter 3:18

Today's Prayer

Lord, let me grow in your wisdom. When I study your Word and follow your commandments, I become a more mature Christian and a more effective servant for you. Let me grow up, Lord, and let me keep growing up every day that I live. Amen.

Patience Builds Character

Be kind to everyone, able to teach, not resentful.

2 Timothy 2:24

The dictionary defines the word *patience* as "the ability to be calm, tolerant, and understanding." For most of us, patience is a hard thing to master. But the Bible teaches that we must learn to wait patiently for the things that God has in store for us, even when waiting is difficult.

In Psalm 37:7, we are commanded to "be still before the Lord and wait patiently for him." But for most of us, waiting patiently for him is difficult. We are fallible human beings who seek solutions to our problems today, not tomorrow. Still, God instructs us to wait patiently for his plans to unfold.

Sometimes, patience is the price we pay for being responsible adults, and that's as it should be. After all, think how patient our heavenly Father has been with us. So the next time you find yourself drumming your fingers as you wait for a quick resolution to the challenges of everyday living, take a deep breath and ask God for patience. Remember that patience builds character . . . and the best moment to start building is this one.

In all negotiations of difficulties, a man may not look to sow and reap at once. He must prepare his business and so ripen it by degrees.

Francis Bacon

He makes us wait. He keeps us in the dark on purpose. He makes us walk when we want to run, sit still when we want to walk, for he has things to do in our souls that we are not interested in.

ELISABETH ELLIOT

As we wait on God, He helps us use the winds of adversity to soar above our problems. As the Bible says, "Those who wait on the LORD . . . shall mount up with wings like eagles."

BILLY GRAHAM

FOR FURTHER REFLECTION

Psalm 27:14; Proverbs 16:32; Lamentations 3:25–26; Romans 8:25; 15:5

Today's Prayer

Heavenly Father, let me wait quietly for you. Let me live according to your plan and according to your timetable. When I am hurried, slow me down. When I become impatient with others, give me empathy. Today, I want to be a patient Christian, dear Lord, as I trust in you and in your master plan. Amen.

You and Your Conscience

Everything that does not come from faith is sin.

Romans 14:23

Billy Graham correctly observed, "Most of us follow our conscience as we follow a wheelbarrow. We push it in front of us in the direction we want to go." To do so, of course, is a profound mistake. Yet all of us, on occasion, have failed to listen to the voice that God planted in our hearts, and all of us have suffered the consequences of our choices.

God gave each of us a conscience for a very good reason: to listen to it. Wise believers make it a practice to listen carefully to that quiet internal voice. Count yourself among that number. When your conscience speaks, listen and learn. In all likelihood, God is trying to get his message through. And in all likelihood, it is a message that you desperately need to hear.

Few things in life torment us more than a guilty conscience. And few things in life provide more contentment than the knowledge that we are obeying God's commandments. A clear conscience is one of the rewards we earn when we obey God's Word and follow his will. When we follow God's will and accept his gift of salvation, our earthly rewards are never ceasing and our heavenly rewards are everlasting.

Today, remember this: the more important the decision, the more carefully you should listen to your conscience.

To go against one's conscience is neither safe nor right. Here I stand. I cannot do otherwise.

MARTIN LUTHER

The convicting work of the Holy Spirit awakens, disturbs, and judges.

FRANKLIN GRAHAM

A quiet conscience sleeps in thunder.

THOMAS FULLER

For Further Reflection

Luke 17:21; Acts 24:16; Romans 12:2;
Colossians 3:1-2; 1 Timothy 1:5

Today's Prayer

Dear Lord, you speak to me through the gift of your Holy Word. And, Father, you speak to me and tell me right from wrong. Let me follow your way, Lord, and, in these quiet moments, show me your plan for this day, that I might serve you. Amen.

Worship Builds Character

Worship the Lord with gladness; come before him with joyful songs. Know that the Lord is God. It is he who made us, and we are his; we are his people, the sheep of his pasture.

Psalm 100:2–3

Some people may tell you that they don't engage in worship. Don't believe them. All of humankind is engaged in worship. The question is not whether we worship but what we worship. Wise men and women choose to worship God. When they do, they are blessed with a plentiful harvest of joy, peace, and abundance.

How can we ensure that we cast our lot with God? We do so, in part, by the practice of regular, purposeful worship in the company of fellow believers. When we worship God faithfully and fervently, we are blessed. When we fail to worship God, for whatever reason, we forfeit the spiritual gifts that might otherwise be ours.

We must worship our heavenly Father, not just with our words, but also with deeds. We must honor him, praise him, and obey him. As we seek to find purpose and meaning for our lives, we must first seek his purpose and his will. For believers, God comes first. Always first.

Worship reminds you of the awesome power of God. So worship him daily, and allow him to work through you every day of the week—not just on Sunday. The best way to worship God is to worship him sincerely and often.

When God is at the center of your life, you worship. When he's not, you worry.

RICK WARREN

Worship is about rekindling an ashen heart into a blazing fire.

LIZ CURTIS HIGGS

Worship is God-centered, aware of one another only in that deep, joyous awareness of being caught up together in God.

ANNE ORTLUND

FOR FURTHER REFLECTION

Matthew 4:10; 6:33; John 4:23–24; 7:37;
Philippians 2:9–11

Today's Prayer

Heavenly Father, let today and every day be a time of worship for me and my family. Let us worship you, not only with words, but also with deeds. In the quiet moments of the day, let us praise you and thank you for creating us, loving us, guiding us, and saving us. Amen.

Kindness Builds Character

Those who are kind benefit themselves,
but the cruel bring ruin on themselves.

Proverbs 11:17

In the busyness and confusion of daily life, it is easy to lose focus, and it is easy to become frustrated. We are imperfect human beings struggling to manage our lives as best we can, but we often fall short. When we are distracted or disappointed, we may neglect to share a kind word or do a kind deed. This oversight hurts others, but it hurts us most of all.

When you weave the thread of kindness into the very fabric of your life, you'll be strengthening your character, but that's not all. You'll also be giving glory to the One who gave his life for you. And as a believer, you must do no less.

Today, slow yourself down and be alert for people who need your smile, your kind words, or your helping hand. Make kindness a centerpiece of your dealings with others. They will be blessed, and you will be, too. Remember: kind words cost nothing, but when they're spoken at the right time, they can be priceless.

Be so preoccupied with good will that you haven't room for ill will.

E. Stanley Jones

When you extend hospitality to others, you're not trying to impress people, you're trying to reflect God to them.

Max Lucado

The mark of a Christian is that he will walk the second mile and turn the other cheek. A wise man or woman gives the extra effort, all for the glory of the Lord Jesus Christ.

John Maxwell

For Further Reflection

Galatians 6:2; Ephesians 4:32; Colossians 3:12; 1 Thessalonians 3:12; 1 Peter 3:8

Today's Prayer

Help me, Lord, to see the needs of those around me. Today, let me show courtesy to those who cross my path. Today, let me spread kind words in honor of your Son. Today, let forgiveness rule my heart. And every day, Lord, let my love for Christ be demonstrated through the acts of kindness that I offer to those who need the healing touch of the Master's hand. Amen.

Making the Most of Mistakes

God chose the foolish things of the world to shame the wise; God chose the weak things of the world to shame the strong.

1 Corinthians 1:27

We are imperfect people living in an imperfect world; mistakes are simply part of the price we pay for being here. But even though mistakes are an inevitable part of life's journey, repeated mistakes should not be. When we commit the inevitable blunders of life, we must correct them, learn from them, and pray for the wisdom not to repeat them. When we do, our mistakes become lessons, and our experiences become adventures in character building.

When our shortcomings are made public, we may feel embarrassed or worse. We may presume (quite incorrectly) that "everybody" is concerned with the gravity of our problem. And as a consequence, we may feel the need to hide from our problems rather than confront them. To do so is wrong. Even when our pride is bruised, we must face up to our mistakes and seek to rise above them.

Here's the big question: have you used your mistakes as stumbling blocks or stepping-stones? The answer to this question will determine how well you perform in the workplace and in every other aspect of your life. So don't let the fear of past failures hold you back. Instead, do the character-building thing: own up to your mistakes and do your best to fix them.

Remember: even if you've make a colossal blunder, God isn't finished with you yet–in fact, he's probably just getting started.

Fix it sooner rather than later: when you make a mistake, the time to make things better is now, not later! The sooner you address your problem, the better.

Truth will sooner come out of error than from confusion.

Francis Bacon

Lord, when we are wrong, make us willing to change; and when we are right, make us easy to live with.

Peter Marshall

I hope you don't mind me telling you all this. One can learn only by seeing one's mistakes.

C. S. Lewis

For Further Reflection

Psalms 40:1–3; 51:1–2; 2 Corinthians 5:17; Ephesians 4:22–24; 1 John 1:9

Today's Prayer

Dear Lord, there's a right way to do things and a wrong way to do things. When I do things that are wrong, help me be quick to ask for forgiveness . . . and quick to correct my mistakes. Amen.

A Life of Integrity

Better the poor whose walk is blameless
than a fool whose lips are perverse.

PROVERBS 19:1

Integrity is built slowly over a lifetime. It is the sum of every right decision and every honest word. It is forged on the anvil of honorable work and polished by the twin virtues of honesty and fairness. Integrity is a precious thing–difficult to build but easy to tear down.

As believers in Christ, we must seek to live each day with discipline, honesty, and faith. When we do, at least two things happen: integrity becomes a habit, and God blesses us because of our obedience to him.

Living a life of integrity isn't always the easiest way, but it is always the right way. God clearly intends that it should be our way, too.

It has been said that character is what we are when nobody is watching. How true. When we do things that we know aren't right, we try to hide them from our families and friends. But even if we successfully conceal our sins from the world, we can never conceal our sins from God.

If you sincerely wish to walk with your Creator, follow his commandments. When you do, your character will take care of itself . . . and you won't need to look over your shoulder to see who, besides God, is watching.

One of your greatest possessions is integrity. Determine today that you will not lose it.

Integrity is not a given factor in everyone's life. It is a result of self-discipline, inner trust, and a decision to be relentlessly honest in all situations in our lives.

JOHN MAXWELL

God doesn't expect you to be perfect, but he does insist on complete honesty.

RICK WARREN

A little lie is like a little pregnancy. It doesn't take long before everyone knows.

C. S. LEWIS

FOR FURTHER REFLECTION

Job 27:5–6; Proverbs 10:9; 11:3; 20:28; Romans 5:3–4

Today's Prayer

Heavenly Father, you instruct your children to seek truth and to live righteously. Help me always to live according to your commandments. Sometimes, Lord, speaking the truth is difficult, but let me always speak truthfully and forthrightly. And let me walk righteously and courageously so that others might see your grace reflected in my words and my deeds. Amen.

God Gives Us Strength

Cast your cares on the Lord *and he will sustain you;*
he will never let the righteous be shaken.

Psalm 55:22

It's a promise that is made over and over again in the Bible: whatever "it" is, God can handle it.

Life isn't always easy. Far from it! Sometimes, life can seem like a long, tiring, character-building, fear-provoking journey. But even when the storm clouds form overhead, even during our darkest moments, we're protected by a loving heavenly Father.

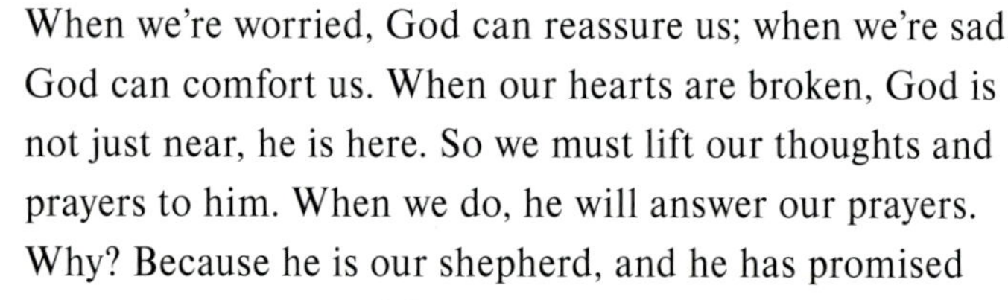

When we're worried, God can reassure us; when we're sad, God can comfort us. When our hearts are broken, God is not just near, he is here. So we must lift our thoughts and prayers to him. When we do, he will answer our prayers. Why? Because he is our shepherd, and he has promised to protect us now and forever.

God's hand uplifts those who turn their hearts and prayers to him.

- Will you count yourself among that number?
- Will you accept God's peace and wear God's armor against the temptations and distractions of our dangerous world?

If you do, you can live courageously and optimistically, knowing that even on the darkest days, you and your heavenly Father can handle every challenge you face today and every day.

Today, think about ways that you can tap into God's strength: start with prayer, worship, and praise.

So rejoice! You are giving Him what He asks you to give Him—the chance to show you what He can do.

AMY CARMICHAEL

By ourselves we are not capable of suffering bravely, but the Lord possesses all the strength we lack and will demonstrate His power when we undergo persecution.

CORRIE TEN BOOM

You may not know what you are going to do; you only know that God knows what He is going to do.

OSWALD CHAMBERS

For Further Reflection

Exodus 15:2; Isaiah 40:29, 31;
Ephesians 6:10; 2 Timothy 2:1

Today's Prayer

Dear Lord, you rule over our world, and I will allow you to rule over my heart. I will obey your commandments, I will study your Word, and I will seek your will for my life today and every day of my life. Amen.

Habits Become Character

Do not be misled: "Bad company corrupts good character."

1 Corinthians 15:33

It's an old saying and a true one: First, you make your habits, and then your habits make you.

- Some habits are character builders, inevitably bringing you closer to God.
- Other habits will lead you away from the path he has chosen for you.

If you sincerely desire to improve your spiritual health, you must honestly examine the habits that make up the fabric of your day. And you must abandon those habits that are displeasing to God.

Perhaps you've tried to become a more disciplined person, but you're still falling back into your old habits. If so, don't get discouraged. Instead, you should become even more determined to evolve into the person God wants you to be.

If you trust God and if you keep asking for his help, he can transform your life. If you sincerely ask him to help you, the same God who created the universe will help you defeat the harmful habits that have heretofore defeated you. So if at first you don't succeed, keep praying. God is listening, and he's ready to help you become a better person if you ask him.

So ask him today.

Target your most unhealthy habit first, and attack it with vigor. When it comes to defeating harmful habitual behaviors, you'll need focus, determination, more focus, and more determination.

You will never change your life until you change something you do daily.

John Maxwell

Since behaviors become habits, make them work with you and not against you.

E. Stanley Jones

Prayer is a habit. Worship is a habit. Kindness is a habit. And if you want to please God, you'd better make sure that these habits are your habits.

Marie T. Freeman

For Further Reflection

Jeremiah 13:23; Ezekiel 33:31; Colossians 3:9–10; Hebrews 10:25; 2 Peter 2:19

Today's Prayer

Dear Lord, help me break bad habits and form good ones. And let my actions be pleasing to you today and every day. Amen.

Listening to Guilt

Therefore, there is now no condemnation for those who are in Christ Jesus.

ROMANS 8:1

If you find yourself plagued by feelings of guilt or shame, consult God's survival guide: his Holy Word. And as you do so, consider the following biblically based tips for overcoming those feeling of guilt once and for all:

1. Ask God for forgiveness. When you ask for it, he will give it (1 John 1:9).

2. Ask forgiveness from the people you have harmed. This step is hard but helpful. And even if the other folks cannot find it in their hearts to forgive you, you have the satisfaction of knowing that you asked (Proverbs 28:13).

3. Forgive yourself. If you're no longer misbehaving, it's the right thing to do. And today is the right day to do it (Romans 14:22).

4. Become more diligent in your daily time of prayer and Bible study. A regular time of quiet reflection and prayer will allow you to praise your Creator, to focus your thoughts, to remind yourself of his love, and to seek his guidance in matters great and small (Isaiah 50:4–5).

5. Get busy making the world a better place. Now that God has forgiven you, it's time for you to show your gratitude by serving him (Matthew 23:11–12).

Feeling guilty? Then stop doing the things that make you feel guilty. How can you expect not to feel guilty if you should feel guilty? (Acts 26:20).

Guilt is a gift that leads us to grace.

FRANKLIN GRAHAM

Identify the sin. Confess it. Turn from it. Avoid it at all costs. Live with a clean, forgiven conscience. Don't dwell on what God has forgotten!

MAX LUCADO

What the devil loves is that vague cloud of unspecified guilt feeling or unspecified virtue by which he lures us into despair or presumption.

C. S. LEWIS

For Further Reflection

Isaiah 43:25; Ephesians 2:4–5; 14:21–22;
2 Timothy 2:15; 1 John 2:28–29

Today's Prayer

Dear Lord, thank you for the guilt that I feel when I disobey you. Help me confess my wrongdoings, help me accept your forgiveness, and help me renew my passion to serve you. Amen.

Perseverance Builds Character

You need to persevere so that when you have done the will of God, you will receive what he has promised.

HEBREWS 10:36

As you continue to seek God's purpose for your life, you will undoubtedly experience your fair share of disappointments, detours, false starts, and failures. When you do, you're facing one of those inevitable tests of character. How should you respond?

The next time you find your courage tested to the limit, remember that God is as near as your next breath, and remember that he offers strength and comfort to his children. He is your shield and your strength; he is your protector and your deliverer. Call upon him in your hour of need and then be comforted. Whatever your challenge, whatever your trouble, God can help you persevere. And that's precisely what he'll do if you ask him.

- Perhaps you are in a hurry for God to help you resolve your difficulties.
- Perhaps you're anxious to earn the rewards that you feel you've already earned from life.
- Perhaps you're drumming your fingers, impatiently waiting for God to act.

If so, be forewarned: God operates on his own timetable, not yours. Sometimes, God may answer your prayers with silence, and when he does, you must patiently persevere. In times of trouble, you must remain steadfast and trust in the merciful goodness of your heavenly Father. Whatever your problem, he can manage it. Your job is to keep persevering until he does.

Are you being tested? Call upon God. God can give you the strength to persevere, and that's exactly what you should ask him to do.

Jesus taught that perseverance is the essential element in prayer.

E. M. Bounds

Perseverance is more than endurance. It is endurance combined with absolute assurance and certainty that what we are looking for is going to happen.

Oswald Chambers

Battles are won in the trenches, in the grit and grime of courageous determination; they are won day by day in the arena of life.

Charles Swindoll

For Further Reflection

2 Chronicles 15:7; 1 Corinthians 9:24–25;
Galatians 6:9; 2 Timothy 4:7; Hebrews 12:1–2

Today's Prayer

Lord, when life is difficult, I am tempted to abandon hope in the future. But you are my God, and I can draw strength from you. Let me trust you, Father, in good times and in bad times. Let me persevere—even if my soul is troubled—and let me follow your Son, Jesus Christ, this day and forever. Amen.

Friends Who Honor God

Greater love has no one than this:
to lay down one's life for one's friends.

John 15:13

If you genuinely want to strengthen your character, you need to build closer relationships with people who want to do the same. That's why fellowship with like-minded believers should be an integral part of your life. Your friendships should be uplifting, enlightening, encouraging, and (above all) character building.

Are your friends the kind of people who encourage you to seek God's will and to obey God's Word? If so, you're choosing your friends wisely.

When you build lasting friendships that are pleasing to God–friendships with godly men and women whose values are admirable and whose intentions are honorable–you will be richly blessed. But if you find yourself spending time with folks whose priorities are as questionable as their ethics, you're treading on dangerous ground. So here's an invaluable tip for character building: be careful–very careful–how you choose your friends.

As you're making friendships, keep these things in mind:

- Be less concerned with appearances and more concerned with integrity.
- Be a trustworthy, encouraging, loyal friend to others.
- Make sure that you appreciate the genuine friends who, by their presence and their love, make you a better person.

Friendship is, after all, a glorious gift, praised by God. Give thanks for that gift and nurture it.

Today, as you think about the nature and the quality of your friendships, remember the first rule of making (and keeping) friends: the Golden Rule. Remember? It starts like this: "Do unto others . . ."

Inasmuch as anyone pushes you nearer to God, he or she is your friend.

BARBARA JOHNSON

Though I know intellectually how vulnerable I am to pride and power, I am the last one to know when I succumb to their seduction. That's why spiritual Lone Rangers are so dangerous–and why we must depend on trusted brothers and sisters who love us enough to tell us the truth.

CHUCK COLSON

My special friends, who know me so well and love me anyway, give me daily encouragement to keep on.

EMILIE BARNES

FOR FURTHER REFLECTION

Proverbs 17:17; 27:17; Philippians 1:3;
1 Peter 3:8; 1 John 4:11

Today's Prayer

Dear Lord, I thank you for my friends. You have brought wonderful Christian friends into my life. Let our friendships honor you as we walk in the footsteps of your Son. Amen.

Enthusiasm, Properly Directed, Builds Character

Whatever you do, work at it with all your heart, as working for the Lord, not for human masters.

COLOSSIANS 3:23

If your zest for life has waned, it is now time to redirect your efforts and recharge your spiritual batteries.

- Are you an enthusiastic person?
- Are you passionate about your faith, your life, your family, and your future?

If you can't truthfully say yes to these questions, it time to refocus your priorities by putting God first.

Each day is a glorious opportunity to serve God and to do his will.

- Are you enthused about life, or do you struggle through each day, giving scarcely a thought to God's blessings?
- Are you constantly praising God for his gifts?
- Are you sharing his Good News with the world?
- Are you excited about the possibilities for service that God has placed before you, whether at home, at work, or at church?

With God's help, you can be and do all of these things.

Don't wait for enthusiasm to find you . . . Go looking for it. Look at your life and your relationships as exciting adventures. Don't wait for life to spice itself; spice things up yourself.

When we wholeheartedly commit ourselves to God, there is nothing mediocre or run-of-the-mill about us. To live for Christ is to be passionate about our Lord and about our lives.

Jim Gallery

Wherever you are, be all there. Live to the hilt every situation you believe to be the will of God.

Jim Elliot

Enthusiasm, like the flu, is contagious–we get it from one another.

Barbara Johnson

For Further Reflection

Ecclesiastes 3:22; 9:10; Romans 12:11;
Ephesians 6:7; 1 Thessalonians 5:16-18

Today's Prayer

Dear Lord, you have called me, not to a life of mediocrity, but to a life of passion. Today, I will be an enthusiastic follower of your Son, and I will share his Good News–and his love–with all who cross my path. Amen.

Do It Now; Build Character Now

When you make a vow to God, do not delay to fulfill it. He has no pleasure in fools; fulfill your vow.

Ecclesiastes 5:4

God calls upon each of us always to act in accordance with his will and with respect for his commandments. To be responsible believers, it is never enough to merely hear God's instructions; we must also live by them (James 1:22). And it is never enough to wait idly by while others do God's work here on Earth; we, too, must act. Doing God's work is a responsibility that each of us must bear, and when we do, we build character moment by moment, day by day.

Are you in the habit of doing what needs to be done when it needs to be done, or are you a dues-paying member of the Procrastinator's Club? If you've acquired the habit of doing things sooner rather than later, congratulations! But if you find yourself putting off all those unpleasant tasks until later (or never), it's time to think about the consequences of your behavior.

One way that you can learn to defeat procrastination is by paying less attention to your fears and more attention to your responsibilities. So when you're faced with a difficult choice or an unpleasant responsibility, don't spend endless hours fretting over your fate. Simply seek God's counsel and get busy. When you do, you will be richly rewarded because of your willingness to act.

Today, pick out one important obligation that you've been putting off. Then, take at least one specific step toward the completion of the task you've been avoiding. Even if you don't finish the job, you'll discover that it's easier to finish a job that you've already begun than to finish a job that you've never started.

Every time you refuse to face up to life and its problems, you weaken your character.

E. Stanley Jones

Now is the only time worth having because, indeed, it is the only time we have.

C. H. Spurgeon

Do noble things, do not dream them all day long.

Charles Kingsley

For Further Reflection

Proverbs 27:12; 1 Corinthians 4:20;
James 1:22; 3:13; 1 Peter 1:13

Today's Prayer

Dear Lord, today is a new day. Help me tackle the important tasks immediately, even if those tasks are unpleasant. Don't let me put off until tomorrow what I should do today. Amen.

Controlling the Direction of Your Thoughts

Do not let wisdom and understanding out of your sight, preserve sound judgment and discretion; they will be life for you.

PROVERBS 3:21–22

Here's a proven way to build character: learn to control the direction of your thoughts. Your thoughts, of course, are intensely powerful things. Your thoughts have the power to lift you up or drag you down; they have the power to energize you or deplete you, to inspire you to greater accomplishments or to make those accomplishments impossible.

How will you and your family members direct your thoughts today? Will you obey the words of Philippians 4:8 by dwelling upon those things that are honorable, true, and worthy of praise? Or will you allow your thoughts to be hijacked by the negativity that seems to dominate our troubled world?

Are you fearful, angry, bored, or worried? Are you so preoccupied with the concerns of this day that you fail to thank God for the promise of eternity? Are you confused, bitter, or pessimistic? If so, God wants to have a little talk with you.

Form the habit of spending more time thinking about your blessings and less time fretting about your hardships. Then, take time to thank the Giver of all things good for gifts that are, in truth, far too numerous to count.

God's cure for evil thinking is to fill our minds with that which is good.

GEORGE SWEETING

Your thoughts are the determining factor as to whose mold you are conformed to. Control your thoughts and you control the direction of your life.

CHARLES STANLEY

If our minds are stayed upon God, His peace will rule the affairs entertained by our minds. If, on the other hand, we allow our minds to dwell on the cares of this world, God's peace will be far from our thoughts.

WOODROLL KROLL

For Further Reflection

Matthew 5:8; Philippians 4:8;
Colossians 2:8; James 4:8; 1 Peter 1:13

Today's Prayer

Dear Lord, I will focus on your love, your power, your promises, and your Son. When I am weak, I will turn to you for strength; when I am worried, I will turn to you for comfort; when I am troubled, I will turn to you for patience and perspective. Help me guard my thoughts, Lord, so that I may honor you this day and forever. Amen.

A Willingness to Serve

You call me "Teacher" and "Lord," and rightly so, for that is what I am. Now that I, your Lord and Teacher, have washed your feet, you also should wash one another's feet. I have set you an example that you should do as I have done for you.

JOHN 13:13–15

We live in a world that glorifies power, prestige, fame, and money. But the words of Jesus teach us that the most esteemed men and women are not the widely acclaimed leaders of society; the most esteemed among us are the humble servants.

Dietrich Bonhoeffer was correct when he observed, "It is very easy to overestimate the importance of our own achievements in comparison with what we owe others." In other words, reality breeds humility . . . and humility should breed service.

Every single day of your life, including this one, God will give you opportunities to serve him by serving other people. Welcome those opportunities with open arms.

Whatever your age, whatever your circumstances, you can serve: each stage of life's journey is a glorious opportunity to place yourself in the service of the One who is the Giver of all blessings. As long as you live, you should honor God with your service to others.

God wants us to serve Him with a willing spirit, one that would choose no other way.

Beth Moore

So many times we say that we can't serve God because we aren't whatever is needed. We're not talented enough or smart enough or whatever. But if you are in covenant with Jesus Christ, He is responsible for covering your weaknesses, for being your strength. He will give you His abilities for your disabilities!

Kay Arthur

God does not do anything with us, only through us.

Oswald Chambers

For Further Reflection

Job 36:11; John 12:26; 1 Corinthians 12:4–5; Hebrews 6:10, 12:28

Today's Prayer

Dear Lord, when Jesus humbled himself and became a servant, he also became an example for me. Make me a faithful steward of my gifts, and let me be a humble servant to my loved ones, to my friends, and to those in need. Amen.

DAY 34

Obedience Builds Character

Not everyone who says to me, "Lord, Lord," will enter the kingdom of heaven, but only the one who does the will of my Father who is in heaven.

Matthew 7:21

Obedience to God is determined, not by words, but by deeds. Talking about righteousness is easy; living righteously is far more difficult, especially in today's temptation-filled world.

Since God created Adam and Eve, we human beings have been rebelling against our Creator. Why? Because we are unwilling to trust God's Word, and we are unwilling to follow his commandments. God has given us a guidebook for righteous living called the Holy Bible. It contains thorough instructions which, if followed, lead to fulfillment, abundance, and salvation. But if we choose to ignore God's commandments, the results are as predictable as they are tragic.

- When we seek righteousness in our own lives–and when we seek the companionship of those who do likewise–we reap rich spiritual rewards.
- When we behave ourselves as godly men and women, we strengthen our character by honoring the Creator.
- When we live righteously and according to God's commandments, he blesses us in ways that we cannot fully understand.

Do you seek God's peace and his blessings? Then obey him.

Obedience leads to spiritual growth. Oswald Chambers correctly observed, "We grow spiritually as our Lord grew physically: by a life of simple, unobtrusive obedience." When you take these words to heart, you will embark upon a lifetime of spiritual growth . . . and God will smile.

All true knowledge of God is born out of obedience.

JOHN CALVIN

Obedience is the outward expression of your love of God.

HENRY BLACKABY

There are two things we are called to do: we are to depend on His strength and be obedient to His Word. If we can't handle being dependent and obedient, we will never become the kind of people who have a heart for God.

STUART BRISCOE

For Further Reflection

Deuteronomy 13:4; 1 Samuel 15:22; Acts 5:29;
1 Peter 1:13–15; 1 John 2:17

Today's Prayer

Lead me along your path, Lord, and guide me far from the frustrations and distractions of this troubled world. Let your Holy Word guide my actions, and let your love reside in my heart this day and every day. Amen.

The Media Tears Down Character

Set your minds on things above, not on earthly things.

Colossians 3:2

Sometimes it's hard to hold on to your integrity, especially when the world keeps pumping out messages that are contrary to your faith and destructive to your character. The media is working around the clock in an attempt to rearrange your priorities.

The media says that the all-important things are:

- Your appearance
- Your possessions
- Fun

But guess what? Those messages are lies. The all-important things in life have to do with your faith, your family, and your future. Period.

Are you willing to make the character-building decision to stand up for your faith? If so, you'll be doing yourself a monumental favor. And consider this: when you begin to speak up for God, isn't it logical to assume that you'll also begin to know him in a more meaningful way? Of course you will.

So forget the media hype, and pay attention to God. Stand up for him and be counted, not just in church where it's relatively easy to be a Christian, but also outside the church, where it's significantly harder. You owe it to God . . . and just as importantly, you owe it to yourself.

Don't trust the media's messages. Many of the messages that you receive from the media are specifically designed to sell you products that interfere with your spiritual, physical, or emotional health. God takes great interest in your health; the moguls from Madison Avenue take great interest in your pocketbook. Trust God.

The more we stuff ourselves with material pleasures, the less we seem to appreciate life.

BARBARA JOHNSON

It is impossible to please God doing things motivated by and produced by the flesh.

BILL BRIGHT

The problem is that the culture seeps into the church, bringing with it a religion without commitment; spirituality without content; aspiration and talk and longing, fulfillment and needs, but not much concern about God.

EUGENE PETERSON

FOR FURTHER REFLECTION

John 15:19; 1 Corinthians 3:18–19;
James 1:27; 1 John 2:15; 5:4

Today's Prayer

Lord, this world is a crazy place, and I have many opportunities to stray from your commandments. Help me to obey you! Let me keep Christ in my heart, and let me put the devil in his place—far away from me! Amen.

Behaving Differently

Let us not become weary in doing good,
for at the proper time we will reap
a harvest if we do not give up.

GALATIANS 6:9

The author of the classic Christian devotional *My Utmost for His Highest*, Oswald Chambers, advised, "Never support an experience which does not have God as its source, and faith in God as its result." These words serve as a powerful reminder that, as Christians, we are called to walk with God and obey his commandments. But we live in a world that presents countless temptations for adults and young people alike.

We Christians, when confronted with sin, have clear instructions: walk–or better yet run–in the opposite direction. When we do, we reap the blessings that God has promised to all those who live according to his will and his word.

Ask yourself if your behavior has been radically changed by your unfolding relationship with God. If the answer to this question is unclear to you–or if the honest answer is a resounding no–think of a single step you can take today, a positive change in your life, that will bring you closer to your Creator.

Although God causes all things to work together for good for His children, He still holds us accountable for our behavior.

KAY ARTHUR

Either God's Word keeps you from sin, or sin keeps you from God's Word.

CORRIE TEN BOOM

The temptation of the age is to look good without being good.

BRENNAN MANNING

For Further Reflection

Proverbs 20:11; Colossians 2:6; James 3:13; 1 Peter 1:14–15; 2 Peter 1:5–6

Today's Prayer

Lord, there is a right way and a wrong way to live. Let me live according to your rules, not the world's rules. Your path is right for me, God; let me follow it every day of my life. Amen.

Doing the Right Thing

Live peaceful and quiet lives
in all godliness and holiness.

1 Timothy 2:2

As Christians, we are called to walk with God and obey his commandments. But our world presents us with countless temptations to stray from God's path. When we honor him by living according to his commandments, we earn for ourselves the abundance and peace that he promises. But when we concern ourselves more with pleasing others than with pleasing our Creator, we bring needless suffering upon ourselves and our families.

Would you like a time-tested formula for successful living? Seek God's approval in every aspect of your life. Does this sound too simple? Perhaps it is simple, but it is also the only way to reap the marvelous riches that God has in store for you.

So today, take every step of your journey with God as your traveling companion. Read his Word and follow his commandments. Support only those activities that further God's kingdom and your spiritual growth. Be an example of righteous living to your friends, to your neighbors, and to your children. Then, reap the blessings that God has promised to all those who live according to his will and his Word.

Today, consider the value of living a life that is pleasing to God. And while you're at it, think about the rewards that are likely to be yours when you do the right thing day in and day out.

The best evidence of our having the truth is our walking in the truth.

Matthew Henry

If we have the true love of God in our hearts, we will show it in our lives. We will not have to go up and down the earth proclaiming it. We will show it in everything we say or do.

D. L. Moody

The purity of motive determines the quality of action.

Oswald Chambers

For Further Reflection

Psalms 92:12; 94:14–15; Matthew 5:8; 6:33; 1 Peter 3:12

Today's Prayer

Holy Father, let my thoughts and my deeds be pleasing to you. I thank you, Lord, for Jesus. Today and every day, I will follow in his footsteps so that my life can be a living testimony to your love, to your forgiveness, and to your Son. Amen.

Generosity Builds Character

Freely you have received; freely give.

MATTHEW 10:8

Every time you give generously to those who need your help, you're strengthening your character. So if you're looking for a surefire way to improve the quality of your life, here it is: be more generous.

The thread of generosity is woven—completely and inextricably—into the very fabric of Christ's teachings. As he sent his disciples out to heal the sick and spread God's message of salvation, Jesus offered this guiding principle: "Freely you have received; freely give" (Matthew 10:8). The principle still applies. If we are to be disciples of Christ, we must give freely of our time, our possessions, and our love.

Paul reminds us that when we sow the seeds of generosity, we reap bountiful rewards in accordance with God's plan for our lives. Thus, we are instructed to give cheerfully and without reservation: "Remember this: Whoever sows sparingly will also reap sparingly, and whoever sows generously will also reap generously. Each of you should give what you have decided in your heart to give, not reluctantly or under compulsion, for God loves a cheerful giver" (2 Corinthians 9: 6-7).

Today, you may feel the urge to hoard your blessings. Don't do it. Instead, give generously to those less fortunate than you. Find a need and fill it. Lend a helping hand and share a word of kindness. It's the godly thing to do—and it's the best way to live.

We can't do everything, but can we do anything more valuable than invest ourselves in another?

Elisabeth Elliot

Generosity is changing one's focus from self to others.

John Maxwell

God does not supply money to satisfy our every whim and desire. His promise is to meet our needs and provide an abundance so that we can help other people.

Larry Burkett

For Further Reflection

Ecclesiastes 11:1; Acts 20:35; 2 Corinthians 9:6–7; Galatians 6:10; 1 Peter 4:10

Today's Prayer

Lord, make me a generous and cheerful Christian. Let me be kind to those who need my encouragement, and let me share with those who need my help today and every day. Amen.

Beyond Discouragement

As for you, be strong and do not give up,
for your work will be rewarded.

2 CHRONICLES 15:7

We live in a world where expectations can be high and demands can be even higher. When we fail to meet the expectations of others—or ourselves—we may be tempted to abandon hope. But God has other plans. He knows exactly how he intends to use us. Our task is to remain faithful.

God offers us strength to meet our challenges, and hope for the future. As a faithful follower of Christ, you have every reason to be hopeful. So if you have become discouraged with the direction of your day or your life, turn your thoughts and prayers to God—and associate with like-minded believers who do the same.

And remember this: your heavenly Father is a God of possibility, not negativity. He is your shepherd; he never leaves your side; and the ultimate victory will be his. So how, then, can you stay discouraged for long?

If you're feeling discouraged, try to redirect your thoughts away from the troubles that plague you; focus, instead, upon the opportunities that surround you.

God does not dispense strength and encouragement like a druggist fills your prescription. The Lord doesn't promise to give us something to take so we can handle our weary moments. He promises us Himself. That is all. And that is enough.

CHARLES SWINDOLL

Feelings of uselessness and hopelessness are not from God, but from the evil one, the devil, who wants to discourage you and thwart your effectiveness for the Lord.

BILL BRIGHT

If I am asked how we are to get rid of discouragements, I can only say, as I have had to say of so many other wrong spiritual habits, we must give them up. It is never worth while to argue against discouragement. There is only one argument that can meet it, and that is the argument of God.

HANNAH WHITALL SMITH

For Further Reflection

Psalm 42:9–11; Isaiah 43:2–3; John 16:33;
2 Corinthians 4:8; James 5:13

Today's Prayer

Heavenly Father, when I am discouraged, I will turn to you, and I will also turn to my Christian friends. I thank you, Father, for friends and family members who are willing to encourage me. I will acknowledge their encouragement, and I will share it. Amen.

Spiritual Warfare

Submit yourselves, then, to God. Resist the devil, and he will flee from you. Come near to God and he will come near to you. Wash your hands, you sinners, and purify your hearts, you double-minded.

JAMES 4:7–8

In his letter to Jewish Christians, Peter offered a stern warning: "Your enemy the devil prowls around like a roaring lion looking for someone to devour" (1 Peter 5:8). What was true in New Testament times is equally true in our own. Evil is indeed abroad in the world, and Satan continues to sow the seeds of destruction far and wide.

In a very real sense, our world is at war:

- Good versus evil
- Sin versus righteousness
- Hope versus suffering
- Praise versus apathy

As Christians, we must ensure that we place ourselves squarely on the right side of these conflicts: God's side. How can we do it?

- By thoughtfully studying God's Word
- By regularly worshiping with fellow believers
- By guarding our hearts and minds against the subtle temptations of the enemy

When we do, we are protected.

It's out there, and it can hurt you. Evil does exist, and you will confront it. Prepare yourself by forming a genuine, life-changing relationship with God and his only begotten Son. There is darkness in this world, but God's light can overpower any darkness.

There is nothing evil in matter itself. Evil lies in the spirit. Evils of the heart, of the mind, of the soul, of the spirit—these have to do with man's sin, and the only reason the human body does evil is because the human spirit uses it to do evil.

A. W. Tozer

There is but one good; that is God. Everything else is good when it looks to Him and bad when it turns from Him.

C. S. Lewis

Rebuke the Enemy in your own name and he laughs; command him in the name of Christ and he flees.

John Eldredge

For Further Reflection

Proverbs 3:7; 4:18–19; Matthew 15:13; John 3:20–21; Romans 12:21

Today's Prayer

Dear Lord, strengthen my walk with you. Sometimes, Father, I need your help to recognize right from wrong. Your presence in my life enables me to choose truth and to live a life that is pleasing to you. May I always live in your presence, and may I walk with you today . . . and forever. Amen.

Walking with the Wise Builds Character

Listen to advice and accept discipline, and at the end you will be among the wise.

Proverbs 19:20

Do you wish to become wise? Then you must walk with people who, by their words and their presence, make you wiser. And, to the best of your ability, you must avoid those people who don't. That means that you must choose wise friends and mentors.

A savvy mentor can help you make character-building choices. And just as importantly, a thoughtful mentor can help you recognize and avoid the hidden big-time mistakes that can derail your day (or your life).

Wise mentors aren't really very hard to find if you look in the right places. So today, as an exercise in character building, select from your friends and family members a mentor whose judgment you trust. Then listen carefully to your mentor's advice and be willing to accept that advice, even if accepting it requires effort or pain or both. Consider your mentor to be God's gift to you. Thank God for that gift and use it.

Rely on the advice of trusted friends and mentors. Proverbs 1:5 makes it clear: "Let the wise listen and add to their learning, and let the discerning get guidance." Do you want to be wise? Starting today, seek counsel from wise people.

The next best thing to being wise oneself is to live in a circle of those who are.

C. S. Lewis

The man who never reads will never be read; he who never quotes will never be quoted. He who will not use the thoughts of other men's brains proves that he has no brains of his own.

C. H. Spurgeon

The effective mentor strives to help a man or woman discover what they can be in Christ and then holds them accountable to become that person.

Howard Hendricks

For Further Reflection

Proverbs 1:5, 7; 14:6–7; 13:20; 14:6–7; 21:20–21

Today's Prayer

Dear Lord, thank you for family members, for friends, and for mentors. When I am troubled, let me turn to them for help, for guidance, for comfort, and for perspective. And, Father, let me be a friend and mentor to others so that my love for you may be reflected in my genuine concern for them. Amen.

You're Accountable

Each one should test their own actions. Then they can take pride in themselves alone, without comparing themselves to someone else, for each one should carry their own load.

Galatians 6:4–5

We humans are masters at passing the buck. Why? Because passing the buck is easier than fixing, and criticizing others is so much easier than improving ourselves. So instead of solving our problems legitimately (by doing the work required to solve them), we are inclined to fret, to blame, and to criticize, while doing precious little else. When we do, our problems, quite predictably, remain unsolved.

Whether you like it or not, you are accountable for your actions. But because you are human, you'll be sorely tempted to pass the blame. Avoid that temptation at all costs.

Problem-solving builds character. Every time you straighten your back and look squarely into the face of Old Man Trouble, you'll strengthen, not only your backbone, but also your spirit. So instead of looking for someone to blame, look for something to fix, and then get busy fixing it.

And as you consider your own situation, remember this: God has a way of helping those who help themselves. But he doesn't spend much time helping those who don't.

It's easy to hold other people accountable, but real accountability begins with the person in the mirror. Think about one specific area of responsibility that is uniquely yours, and think about a specific step you can take today to better fulfill that responsibility.

Generally speaking, accountability is a willingness to share our activities, conduct, and fulfillment of assigned responsibilities with others.

CHARLES STANLEY

We urgently need people who encourage and inspire us to move toward God and away from the world's enticing pleasures.

JIM CYMBALA

The Bible teaches that we are accountable to one another for our conduct and character.

CHARLES STANLEY

FOR FURTHER REFLECTION

Deuteronomy 6:18; Psalm 97:11-12;
Proverbs 2:20-22; 20:11; Jeremiah 17:10

Today's Prayer

Lord, I want to stand behind the things I do. Let me not pass the buck or assign blame to others. Instead, let me be an example to others through my hard work and dedication to doing what's right today and every day. Amen.

Sloth Destroys Character

One thing I do: Forgetting what is behind and straining toward what is ahead, I press on toward the goal to win the prize for which God has called me heavenward in Christ Jesus.

PHILIPPIANS 3:13–14

Perhaps you've heard it said: "Give the boss an honest day's work for an honest day's pay." But sometimes, you'll be tempted to do otherwise. From time to time, you'll become upset with your job, and it is during these times, when you're frustrated or upset, that you'll be tempted to gripe, to waste time, and to do little else. Avoid these temptations—they're self-destructive.

Even if you're planning on quitting your job tomorrow, give your boss a full day's work today. Otherwise, you'll be developing a very bad habit: the habit of giving less than 100 percent. It's a character-destroying trait—an easy habit to acquire and a difficult habit to break.

If you're looking for folks with whom to waste time, you can probably find them just about anywhere—including your workplace. But if you're looking for a meaningful life and a career that you love, make up your mind to be the kind of person whose work speaks for itself. When you do, you'll discover that when you give your best, you enjoy work the most.

Feeling a little lazy? That means that you're not excited about your work. So here's your challenge: find work that's so much fun you can't wait to clock in. When you do, you'll discover that a really good job beats leisure (or unemployment) hands down.

The worst thing that laziness does is rob a man of spiritual purpose.

BILLY GRAHAM

The only cure for laziness is to be filled with the life of God.

OSWALD CHAMBERS

Idleness is the enemy of the soul.

ST. BENEDICT OF NURSIA

FOR FURTHER REFLECTION

2 Chronicles 31:21; Proverbs 21:25–26; Ecclesiastes 9:10; John 9:4; Ephesians 6:6–7

Today's Prayer

Lord, I know that you desire a bountiful harvest for all your children. But you have instructed us that we must sow before we reap, not after. Help me, Lord, to sow the seeds of your abundance everywhere I go. Let me be diligent in all my undertakings and give me patience to wait for your harvest. In time, Lord, let me reap the harvest that is found in your will for my life. Amen.

Trusting God's Promises

Let us hold unswervingly to the hope we profess,
for he who promised is faithful.

Hebrews 10:23

What do you expect from the day ahead? Are you willing to trust God completely, or are you living beneath a cloud of doubt and fear? God's Word makes it clear: you should trust him and his promises, and when you do, you can live courageously.

For thoughtful Christians, every day begins and ends with God's Son and God's promises. When we accept Christ into our hearts, God promises us the opportunity for earthly peace and spiritual abundance. But more importantly, God promises us the priceless gift of eternal life.

Sometimes, especially when we find ourselves caught in the inevitable entanglements of life, we fail to trust God completely.

- Are you tired? Discouraged? Fearful? Be comforted and trust the promises that God has made to you.
- Are you worried or anxious? Be confident in God's power.
- Do you see a difficult future ahead? Be courageous and call upon God. He will protect you and then use you according to his purposes.
- Are you confused? Listen to the quiet voice of your heavenly Father.

Do you really trust God's promises, or are you hedging your bets? Today, think about the role that God's Word plays in your life, and think about ways that you can worry less and trust God more.

The stars may fall, but God's promises will stand and be fulfilled.

J. I. Packer

We honor God by asking for great things when they are a part of His promise. We dishonor Him and cheat ourselves when we ask for molehills where He has promised mountains.

Vance Havner

God's promises are overflowings from his great heart.

C. H. Spurgeon

For Further Reflection

Psalms 18:30; 119:116;
Hebrews 6:11–12, 17–18; 10:36

Today's Prayer

Lord, your Holy Word contains promises, and I will trust them. I will use the Bible as my guide. I will trust you, Lord, to speak to me through your Holy Spirit and through your Holy Word this day and forever. Amen.

Real Transformation? Inner Transformation!

Therefore, if anyone is in Christ, the new creation has come: The old has gone, the new is here!

2 Corinthians 5:17

Have you invited God's Son to reign over your heart and your life? If so, think for a moment about the old you, the person you were before you invited Christ into your heart. Now, think about the new you, the person you have become since then. Is there a difference between the old you and the "new and improved" version? There should be! And that difference should be noticeable not only to you but also to others.

Warren Wiersbe observed, "The greatest miracle of all is the transformation of a lost sinner into a child of God." And Oswald Chambers noted, "If the Spirit of God has transformed you within, you will exhibit Divine characteristics in your life, not good human characteristics. God's life in us expresses itself as God's life, not as a human life trying to be godly."

When you invited Christ to reign over your heart, you became a new creation through him. This day offers yet another opportunity to behave yourself like that new creation by serving your Creator and strengthening your character. When you do, God will guide your steps and bless your endeavors today and forever.

Today, remember this: a true conversion experience results in a life transformed by Christ and a commitment to following in his footsteps.

No man is ever the same after God has laid His hand upon him.

A. W. Tozer

Being born again is God's solution to our need for love and life and light.

Anne Graham Lotz

Conversion is not a blind leap into the darkness. It is a joyous leap into the light that is the love of God.

Corrie ten Boom

For Further Reflection

Matthew 18:2-3; John 3:3-5; Romans 6:4;
Ephesians 4:22-24; 1 John 5:1

Today's Prayer

Lord, when I accepted Jesus as my personal Savior, you changed me forever and made me whole. Let me share your Son's message with my friends, with my family, and with the world. You are a God of love, redemption, conversion, and salvation. I will praise you today and forever. Amen.

Materialism Tears Down Character

Do not store up for yourselves treasures on earth, where moths and vermin destroy, and where thieves break in and steal. But store up for yourselves treasures in heaven, where moths and vermin do not destroy, and where thieves do not break in and steal. For where your treasure is, there your heart will be also.

MATTHEW 6:19–21

Whenever we place our love for material possessions above our love for God, we find ourselves engaged in a struggle between good and evil. Respond to this struggle by simplifying your life and improving your world.

Learn to control your possessions before they control you:

- Purchase only those things that make a significant contribution to your well-being and the well-being of your family.
- Never spend more than you make.
- Understand the folly in buying consumer goods on credit.
- Never use credit cards as a way of financing your lifestyle.

Ask yourself this simple question: "Do I own my possessions, or do they own me?" If you don't like your answer, stop acquiring and start divesting. You'll be pleasantly surprised at the sense of satisfaction that accompanies your newfound moderation. And you'll understand firsthand that when it comes to material possessions, less truly is more.

Genuine happiness comes not from money but from the things that money can't buy—starting, of course, with your relationship to God and his only begotten Son.

When possessions become our god, we become materialistic and greedy . . . and we forfeit our contentment and our joy.

Charles Swindoll

He is no fool who gives what he cannot keep to gain what he cannot lose.

Jim Elliot

As faithful stewards of what we have, ought we not to give earnest thought to our staggering surplus?

Elisabeth Elliot

For Further Reflection

Proverbs 11:28; Mark 8:36-37; Luke 12:34;
1 Timothy 6:7-8; 1 John 2:15

Today's Prayer

Lord, my greatest possession is my relationship with you through Jesus Christ. You have promised that when I first seek your kingdom and your righteousness, you will give me whatever I need. Let me trust you completely, Lord, for my needs—both material and spiritual—this day and always. Amen.

Need Something from God? Ask!

You do not have because you do not ask God.

James 4:2

Jesus made it clear to his disciples: they should petition God to meet their needs. So should you. Genuine, heartfelt prayer produces powerful changes in you and in your world. When you lift your heart to God, you open yourself to a never-ending source of divine wisdom and infinite love.

James 5:16 makes a promise that God intends to keep: “The prayer of a righteous person is powerful and effective.” Too many people, however, are too timid or too pessimistic to ask God to do big things. Please don’t count yourself among their number.

God can do great things through you if you have the courage to ask him (and the determination to keep asking him). But don’t expect him to do all the work. When you do your part, he will do his part—and when he does, you can expect miracles to happen.

Today, think of a specific need that is weighing heavily on your heart. Then, spend a few quiet moments asking God for his guidance and for his help.

We get into trouble when we think we know what to do and we stop asking God if we're doing it.

STORMIE OMARTIAN

God makes prayer as easy as possible for us. He's completely approachable and available, and He'll never mock or upbraid us for bringing our needs before Him.

SHIRLEY DOBSON

Often I have made a request of God with earnest pleadings even backed up with Scripture, only to have Him say "No" because He had something better in store.

RUTH BELL GRAHAM

For Further Reflection

Luke 11:9, 11–13; John 15:7; 16:23–24; Philippians 4:6

Today's Prayer

Lord, today I will ask you for the things I need. In every situation, I will come to you in prayer. You know what I want, Lord, and more importantly, you know what I need. Yet even though I know that you know, I still won't be too timid–or too busy–to ask. Amen.

Using the Talents God Gave You

I remind you to fan into flame
the gift of God, which is in you.

2 Timothy 1:6

All of us have special talents, and you are no exception. But your talent is no guarantee of success. It must be cultivated and nurtured; otherwise, it will go unused . . . and God's gift to you will be squandered.

In the twenty-fifth chapter of Matthew, Jesus tells the parable of the talents. In it, he describes a master who leaves his servants with varying amounts of money (talents). When the master returns, some servants have put their money to work and earned more, to which the master responds, "Well done, good and faithful servant! You have been faithful with a few things; I will put you in charge of many things. Come and share your master's happiness!" (Matthew 25:21).

But the story does not end so happily for the foolish servant who was given a single talent but did nothing with it. For this man, the master has nothing but reproach: "You wicked, lazy servant!" (Matthew 25:26). The message from Jesus is clear: We must use our talents, not waste them.

Your particular talent is a treasure on temporary loan from God. He intends that your talent enrich the world and enrich your life. Value the gift that God has given you, nourish it, make it grow, and share it with the world. Then, when you meet your Master face-to-face, you, too, will hear those wonderful words, "Well done, good and faithful servant! . . . Come and share your Master's happiness!"

Converting raw talent into polished skill usually requires work–and lots of it. God's Word clearly instructs you to do the hard work of refining your talents for the glory of his kingdom and the service of his people. It's up to you to make sure that your gift is worthy of the Giver.

God often reveals His direction for our lives through the way He made us . . . with a certain personality and unique skills.

Bill Hybels

Employ whatever God has entrusted you with, in doing good, all possible good, in every possible kind and degree.

John Wesley

What we are is God's gift to us. What we become is our gift to God.

Anonymous

For Further Reflection

Matthew 25:20–21; Romans 12:6–8; Ephesians 4:11–16; 1 Corinthians 12:4–5; 1 Peter 4:10–11

Today's Prayer

Dear Lord, let me use my gifts, and let me help others discover theirs. Your gifts are priceless and eternal. May we, as your faithful children, use our own gifts to the glory of your kingdom today and forever. Amen.

Value-Based Decisions

Live lives worthy of God, who calls you into his kingdom and glory.

1 Thessalonians 2:12

Society seeks to impose its set of values upon you; however, these values are often contrary to God's Word (and thus contrary to your own best interests). The world makes promises that it simply cannot fulfill. It promises happiness, contentment, prosperity, and abundance. But genuine abundance is not a by-product of possessions or status; it is a by-product of your thoughts, your actions, and your relationship with God. The world's promises are incomplete and deceptive; God's promises are unfailing. Your challenge, then, is to build your value system upon the firm foundation of God's promises—nothing else will suffice.

Do you want to strengthen your character? If so, then you must build your life upon a value system that puts God first. So when you're faced with a difficult choice or a powerful temptation, seek God's counsel and trust the counsel that he gives. Invite God into your heart and live according to his commandments. Study his Word and talk to him often. When you do, you will share in the abundance and peace that only God can give.

Whose values will you share? You can have the values that the world holds dear, or you can have the values that God holds dear, but you can't have both. The decision is yours . . . and so are the consequences.

As the first community to which a person is attached and the first authority under which a person learns to live, the family establishes society's most basic values.

Chuck Colson

Education without values, as useful as it is, seems rather to make man a more clever devil.

C. S. Lewis

If you want to be proactive in the way you live your life, if you want to influence your life's direction, if you want your life to exhibit the qualities you find desirable, and if you want to live with integrity, then you need to know what your values are, decide to embrace them, and practice them every day.

John Maxwell

For Further Reflection

Matthew 6:1-2, 24; Luke 6:32-42;
James 1:22-27; 2:14-24

Today's Prayer

Lord, help me value the things in this world that are really valuable: my life, my family, and my relationship with you. Amen.

Strong Enough to Encourage Others

Let us consider how we may spur one another on toward love and good deeds, not giving up meeting together, as some are in the habit of doing, but encouraging one another–and all the more as you see the Day approaching.

Hebrews 10:24–25

In his letter to the Ephesians, Paul writes, "Do not let any unwholesome talk come out of your mouths, but only what is helpful for building others up according to their needs, that it may benefit those who listen" (4:29). As Christians, God wants us to choose our words carefully so as to build others up through wholesome, honest encouragement.

As a faithful follower of Jesus, you have every reason to be hopeful, and you have every reason to share your hopes with others. When you do, you will discover that hope, like other human emotions, is contagious.

So do the world (and yourself) a favor: look for the good in others and celebrate the good that you find. When you do, you'll be a powerful force of encouragement to your friends and family . . . and a worthy servant to your God.

Do you want to be successful? Encourage others to do the same. You can't lift other people up without lifting yourself up, too. And remember the words of Oswald Chambers: "God grant that we may not hinder those who are battling their way slowly into the light."

Do you wonder where you can go for encouragement and motivation? Run to Jesus.

MAX LUCADO

A lot of people have gone further than they thought they could because someone else thought they could.

ZIG ZIGLAR

As you're rushing through life, take time to stop a moment, look into people's eyes, say something kind, and try to make them laugh!

BARBARA JOHNSON

FOR FURTHER REFLECTION

Proverbs 12:25; 27:17; Galatians 6:2; Colossians 2:2; Hebrews 3:13

Today's Prayer

Dear Lord, make me a person who is quick to celebrate the accomplishments of others. Make me a source of genuine, lasting encouragement to my family and friends. And let my words and deeds be worthy of your Son, the One who gives me strength and salvation, this day and for all eternity. Amen.

Beyond Excuses

Let us behave decently. . . . Clothe yourselves with the Lord Jesus Christ, and do not think about how to gratify the desires of the flesh.

Romans 13:13–14

All too often we are quick to proclaim ourselves victims, and we refuse to take responsibility for our actions. So we make excuses, excuses, and more excuses—with predictably poor results.

We live in a world where excuses are everywhere. And it's precisely because excuses are so numerous that they are also so ineffective. When we hear the words "I'm sorry but . . .", most of us know exactly what is to follow: an excuse.

- The dog ate the homework.
- Traffic was terrible.
- It's the company's fault.
- The boss is to blame.
- The equipment is broken.
- We're out of that.

And so forth and so on.

Because we humans are such creative excuse-makers, all of the really good excuses have already been taken. In fact, the high-quality excuses have been used, re-used, overused, and abused. That's why excuses don't work—we've heard them all before.

So if you're wasting your time trying to portray yourself as a victim (and weakening your character in the process) or if you're trying to concoct a new and improved excuse, don't bother. Excuses don't work, and while you're inventing them, neither do you.

Today, think of something important that you've been putting off. Then, think of the excuses you've used to avoid that responsibility. Finally, ask yourself, "What can I do today to finish the work I've been avoiding?"

Replace your excuses with fresh determination.

Charles Swindoll

We need to stop focusing on our lacks and stop giving out excuses and start looking at and listening to Jesus.

Anne Graham Lotz

An excuse is only the skin of a reason stuffed with a lie.

Vance Havner

For Further Reflection

Psalm 141:4; John 15:22; Romans 3:19; Galatians 6:7; 1 Peter 2:16

Today's Prayer

Heavenly Father, how easy it is to make excuses. But I want to be a person who accomplishes important work for you. Help me, Father, to strive for excellence, not excuses. Amen.

Beyond Worry

Do not let your hearts be troubled.
You believe in God; believe also in me.

JOHN 14:1

Because you have the ability to think, you also have the ability to worry. Perhaps you are concerned about your future, your relationships, or your finances. Or perhaps you are simply a worrier by nature. If so, choose to make verses from Matthew 6 a regular part of your daily Bible reading:

> *Therefore I tell you, do not worry about your life, what you will eat or drink; or about your body, what you will wear. Is not life more than food, and the body more than clothes? Look at the birds of the air; they do not sow or reap or store away in barns, and yet your heavenly Father feeds them. Are you not much more valuable than they? Can any one of you by worrying add a single hour to your life? Therefore do not worry about tomorrow, for tomorrow will worry about itself. Each day has enough trouble of its own* (6:25–27, 34).

This beautiful passage reminds you that God still sits in his heaven, and you are his beloved child. Because God is trustworthy, perhaps you will worry a little less and trust God a little more, knowing that you are protected.

Divide your areas of concern into two categories: those you can control and those you cannot. Resolve never to waste time or energy worrying about the latter.

Much that worries us beforehand can, quite unexpectedly, have a happy and simple solution. Worries just don't matter. Things really are in a better hand than ours.

DIETRICH BONHOEFFER

Today is mine. Tomorrow is none of my business. If I peer anxiously into the fog of the future, I will strain my spiritual eyes so that I will not see clearly what is required of me now.

ELISABETH ELLIOTT

The beginning of anxiety is the end of faith, and the beginning of true faith is the end of anxiety.

GEORGE MUELLER

For Further Reflection

Psalm 94:19; Proverbs 12:25; Matthew 6:31-34; 11:28-30; Philippians 4:6-7

Today's Prayer

Dear Lord, wherever I find myself, let me celebrate more and worry less. When my faith begins to waver, help me to trust you more. Then, with praise on my lips and the love of your Son in my heart, let me live courageously, faithfully, prayerfully, and thankfully this day and every day. Amen.

Too Many Distractions?

Let us throw off everything that hinders and the sin that so easily entangles. And let us run with perseverance the race marked out for us, fixing our eyes on Jesus, the pioneer and perfecter of faith.

Hebrews 12:1–2

All of us must live through those days when the traffic jams, the computer crashes, and the dog makes a main course out of our homework. But when we find ourselves distracted by the minor frustrations of life, we must catch ourselves, take a deep breath, and lift our thoughts upward.

Although we must sometimes struggle mightily to rise above the distractions of everyday living, we need never struggle alone. God is here—eternal and faithful, with infinite patience and love; and if we reach out to him, he will restore our sense of perspective and give peace to our hearts.

Today, as an exercise in character building, make this promise to yourself and keep it: promise to focus your thoughts on things that are really important—things like your faith, your family, your friends, and your future. Don't allow the day's interruptions to derail your most important work. And don't allow other people (or, for that matter, the media) to decide what's important to you and your family.

Distractions are everywhere, but, thankfully, so is God—and that fact has everything to do with how you prioritize your day and your life.

Take a few minutes to consider the everyday distractions that are interfering with your life and your faith. Then, jot down at least three ideas for minimizing those distractions or eliminating them altogether.

Setting goals is one way you can be sure that you will focus your efforts on the main things so that trivial matters will not become your focus.

Charles Stanley

When Jesus is in our midst, he brings His limitless power along as well. But, Jesus must be in the middle, all eyes and hearts focused on Him.

Shirley Dobson

There is an enormous power in little things to distract our attention from God.

Oswald Chambers

For Further Reflection

Mark 4:19; Luke 8; Romans 12:2;
1 Corinthians 7:35; 1 John 2:15

Today's Prayer

Dear Lord, help me to face this day with a spirit of optimism and thanksgiving. And let me focus my thoughts on you and your incomparable gifts. Amen.

Your Character, Your Family

Choose for yourselves this day whom you will serve. . . .
As for me and my household, we will serve the Lord.

Joshua 24:15

You live in a fast-paced, demanding world, a place where life can be difficult and pressures can be intense. Even when the demands of everyday life are great, you must never forget that you have been entrusted with a profound responsibility—the responsibility to contribute to your family's emotional and spiritual well-being. It's a big job, but with God's help, you're up to the task.

When you place God squarely in the center of your family's life—when you worship him, praise him, trust him, and love him—then he will most certainly bless you and yours in ways that you could have scarcely imagined.

So the next time your family life becomes a little stressful, remember this: your little band of men, women, kids, and babies is a priceless treasure on temporary loan from the Father above. And it's your responsibility to praise God for that gift—and to act accordingly.

Today, think about the importance of saying yes to your family, even if it means saying no to other obligations.

When you think about it for a moment, it certainly makes sense that if people can establish a loving and compatible relationship at home, they have a better chance of establishing winning relationships with those with whom they work on a regular basis.

Zig Ziglar

You cannot honor your family without nurturing you own sense of personal value and honor.

Stephen Covey

When God asks someone to do something for Him entailing sacrifice, He makes up for it in surprising ways. Though He has led Bill all over the world to preach the gospel, He has not forgotten the little family in the mountains of North Carolina.

Ruth Bell Graham

For Further Reflection

Proverbs 11:29; Mark 3:24-25;
Romans 12:9-10; 1 Timothy 5:4, 8

Today's Prayer

Dear Lord, I am part of your family, and I praise you for your gifts and your love. Father, you have also blessed me with my earthly family. Let me show love and acceptance for my own family so that through me, they might come to know you. Amen.

Taking Time to Praise God

I will give thanks to you, Lord, with all my heart; I will tell of all your wonderful deeds. I will be glad and rejoice in you; I will sing the praises of your name, O Most High.

Psalm 9:1–2

If you'd like to strengthen your character, spend more time praising God. And when, by the way, is the best time to praise God?

- In church?
- Before dinner is served?
- When we tuck little children into bed?

None of the above. The best time to praise God is all day, every day, to the greatest extent we can, with thanksgiving in our hearts.

Too many of us, even well-intentioned believers, tend to compartmentalize our waking hours into a few familiar categories: work, rest, play, family time, and worship. To do so is a mistake. Worship and praise should be woven into the fabric of everything we do; it should never be relegated to a weekly three-hour visit to church on Sunday morning. Today, find a little more time to lift your concerns to God in prayer, and praise him for all that he has done. He's listening . . . and he wants to hear from you.

Remember that it always pays to praise your Creator. That's why thoughtful believers (like you) make it a habit to praise God all day, every day.

Praise opens the window of our hearts, preparing us to walk more closely with God. Prayer raises the window of our spirit, enabling us to listen more clearly to the Father.

Max Lucado

Nothing we do is more powerful or more life-changing than praising God.

Stormie Omartian

Worship is an act which develops feelings for God, not a feeling for God which is expressed in an act of worship. When we obey the command to praise God in worship, our deep, essential need to be in relationship with God is nurtured.

Eugene Peterson

For Further Reflection

1 Chronicles 16:28; Psalm 75:1; Jeremiah 20:13; Daniel 2:20; Hebrews 13:15

Today's Prayer

Heavenly Father, I come to you today with hope in my heart and praise on my lips. Make me a faithful steward of the blessings you have entrusted to me. Let me follow in Christ's footsteps today and every day that I live. And let my words and deeds praise you now and forever. Amen.

Society's Treasures

If you belonged to the world, it would love you as its own. As it is, you do not belong to the world, but I have chosen you out of the world. That is why the world hates you.

JOHN 15:19

All of humankind is engaged in a colossal, worldwide treasure hunt. Some people seek treasure from earthly sources–treasures such as material wealth or public acclaim; others seek God's treasures by making him the cornerstone of their lives.

What kind of treasure hunter are you? Are you so caught up in the demands of everyday living that you sometimes allow the search for worldly treasures to become your primary focus? If so, it's time to reorganize your daily to-do list by placing God in his rightful place: first place. Don't allow anyone or anything to separate you from your heavenly Father and his only begotten Son.

The world's treasures are difficult to find and difficult to keep; God's treasures are ever present and everlasting. Which treasures, then, will you claim as your own?

If you're determined to be a faithful follower of the One from Galilee, you must make certain that you focus on his values, not society's values (and by the way, those two sets of values are almost never the same).

Because the world is deceptive, it is dangerous. The world can even deceive God's own people and lead them into trouble.

WARREN WIERSBE

Give me Your grace, good Lord, to count the world as nothing; to set my mind firmly on You and not to hang on the blasting words of men's mouths.

ST. THOMAS MORE

A fish would never be happy living on land, because it was made for water. An eagle could never feel satisfied if it wasn't allowed to fly. You will never feel completely satisfied on earth, because you were made for more.

RICK WARREN

FOR FURTHER REFLECTION

Matthew 6:19–21, 24; Hebrews 13:5;
1 Timothy 6:10; 1 John 2:15–17

Today's Prayer

Lord, this world is a crazy place, and I have many opportunities to stray from your commandments. Help me turn to obey you! Let me keep Christ in my heart, and let me put the devil in his place: far away from me! Amen.

Seeking God's Plans

"For I know the plans I have for you," declares the LORD, *"plans to prosper you and not to harm you, plans to give you hope and a future."*

JEREMIAH 29:11

At times, you may be confident that you are doing God's will. But on other occasions, you may be uncertain about the direction that your life should take. At times, you may wander aimlessly in a wilderness of your own making. And sometimes, you may struggle mightily against God in a vain effort to find success and happiness through your own means, not his.

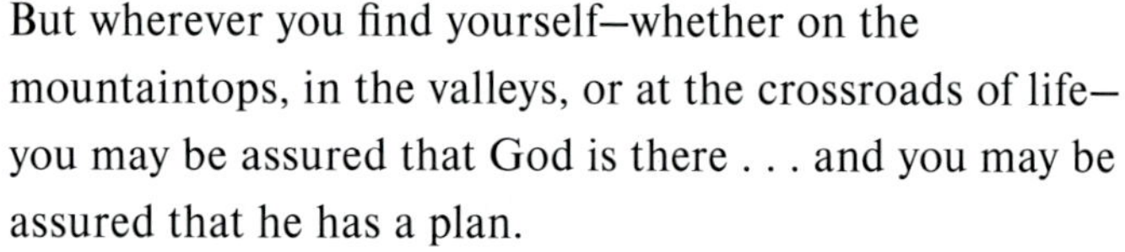

But wherever you find yourself—whether on the mountaintops, in the valleys, or at the crossroads of life—you may be assured that God is there . . . and you may be assured that he has a plan.

When you arrive at one of life's inevitable crossroads, that's the moment when you should turn your thoughts and prayers toward God. When you do, he will make himself known to you in a time and manner of his choosing. When you discover God's plan for your life, you will experience abundance, peace, joy, and power—God's power.

And that's the only kind of power that really matters.

God has a wonderful plan for your life. And the time to start looking for that plan—and living it—is now. And remember: discovering God's plan begins with prayer, but it doesn't end there. You've also got to work at it.

One of the wonderful things about being a Christian is the knowledge that God has a plan for our lives.

Warren Wiersbe

A saint's life is in the hands of God just as a bow and arrow are in the hands of an archer. God is aiming at something the saint cannot see.

Oswald Chambers

In God's plan, God is the standard for perfection. We don't compare ourselves to others; they are just as fouled up as we are. The goal is to be like him; anything less is inadequate.

Max Lucado

For Further Reflection

Genesis 50:20; Psalm 143:10; Proverbs 16:9;
Isaiah 55:8–9; Romans 8:28

Today's Prayer

Dear Lord, I will earnestly seek your will for my life. You have a plan for me that I can never fully understand. But you understand. And I will trust you today, tomorrow, and forever. Amen.

Money: Tool or Master?

For the love of money is a root of all kinds of evil. Some people, eager for money, have wandered away from the faith and pierced themselves with many griefs.

1 Timothy 6:10

Here's a scary thought: the content of your character is demonstrated by the way you choose to spend money. If you spend money wisely and if you give God his fair share, then you're doing just fine. But if you're up to your eyeballs in debt and if "Shop till you drop" is your unofficial motto, it's time to retire the credit cards and rearrange your priorities.

Our society is in love with money and the things that money can buy. God is not. God cares about people, not possessions, and so must we. We must, to the best of our abilities, love our neighbors as ourselves; and we must, to the best of our abilities, resist the mighty temptation to place possessions ahead of people.

Money, in and of itself, is not evil; worshiping money is. So today, as you prioritize matters of importance for you and yours, remember that God is almighty, but the dollar is not.

Are you choosing to make money your master? If so, it's time to turn your thoughts and your prayers to more important matters. And it's time to begin storing up riches that will endure throughout eternity: the spiritual kind.

Put God where he belongs: first. Any relationship that doesn't honor God is a relationship that is destined for problems—and that includes your relationship with money. So spend (and save) accordingly.

Servants of God are always more concerned about ministry than money.

RICK WARREN

No man can stand in front of Jesus Christ and say "I want to make money."

OSWALD CHAMBERS

Have you prayed about your resources lately? Find out how God wants you to use your time and your money. No matter what it costs, forsake all that is not of God.

KAY ARTHUR

For Further Reflection

Proverbs 22:7; Ecclesiastes 5:10; Matthew 6:24; Hebrews 13:5; 1 Peter 4:10

Today's Prayer

Dear Lord, help me to think sensibly about money. And let me always remember that my greatest possession has nothing to do with my checkbook; my greatest possession is my relationship with you through Jesus Christ. Amen.

Emotions: Who's in Charge of Yours?

Make every effort to add to your faith goodness; and to goodness, knowledge; and to knowledge, self-control; and to self-control, perseverance; and to perseverance, godliness; and to godliness, mutual affection; and to mutual affection, love.

2 Peter 1:5–7

Hebrews 10:38 teaches that we should live by faith: "My righteous one will live by faith. And I take no pleasure in the one who shrinks back." Yet sometimes, despite our best intentions, negative feelings can rob us of the great peace and abundance that would otherwise be ours through Christ. When anger or anxiety separates us from the spiritual blessings that God has in store, we must rethink our priorities and renew our faith.

And we must place faith above feelings. Human emotions are highly variable, decidedly unpredictable, and often unreliable. Our emotions are like the weather, only far more fickle. So we must learn to live by faith, not by the ups and downs of our own emotional roller coasters.

Sometime today, you will probably be gripped by a strong negative emotion.

- Distrust it.
- Reign it in.
- Test it.
- And turn it over to God.

Your emotions will inevitably change; God will not. So trust him completely as you watch your negative feelings slowly evaporate into thin air—which, of course, they will.

Remember: your life shouldn't be ruled by your emotions; your life should be ruled by God. So if you think you've lost control over your emotions, don't make big decisions, don't strike out against anybody, and don't speak out in anger. Count to ten (or more) and take time out from your situation until you calm down.

Our feelings do not affect God's facts.

AMY CARMICHAEL

The only serious mistake we can make is the mistake that Psalm 121 prevents: the mistake of supposing that God's interest in us waxes and wanes in response to our spiritual temperature.

EUGENE PETERSON

I may no longer depend on pleasant impulses to bring me before the Lord. I must rather respond to principles I know to be right, whether I feel them to be enjoyable or not.

JIM ELLIOT

For Further Reflection

Proverbs 12:25; 15:13–15; 16:32; 17:22; John 14:1

Today's Prayer

Heavenly Father, you are my strength and my refuge. As I journey through this day, I will encounter events that cause me emotional distress. Lord, when I am troubled, let me turn to you. Keep me steady, Lord, and in those difficult moments, renew a right spirit inside my heart. Amen.

The Character-Building Path: Following God's Footsteps

"Come, follow me," Jesus said, "and I will send you out to fish for people." At once they left their nets and followed him.

Mark 1:17–18

Jesus walks with you. Are you walking with him? Hopefully, you will choose to walk with him today and every day of your life.

Jesus loves you so much that he endured unspeakable humiliation and suffering for you. How will you respond to Christ's sacrifice? Will you take up his cross and follow him (Luke 9:23), or will you choose another path? When you place your hopes squarely at the foot of the cross, when you place Jesus squarely at the center of your life, you will be blessed.

An old familiar hymn begins "What a friend we have in Jesus." No truer words were ever penned. Jesus is the sovereign friend and ultimate Savior of humankind. Christ showed enduring love for his believers by willingly sacrificing his own life so that we might have eternal life. Now, it is our turn to become his friend.

Let us love our Savior, let us praise him, and let us share his message of salvation with the world. When we do, we demonstrate that our acquaintance with the Master is not a passing fancy but is, instead, the cornerstone and the touchstone of our lives.

Following Christ is a matter of obedience. If you want to be a little more like Jesus:

- Learn about his teachings.
- Follow in his footsteps.
- Obey his commandments.

Imagine the spiritual strength the disciples drew from walking hundreds of miles with Jesus.

John Maxwell

It's your heart that Jesus longs for: your will to be made His own with self on the cross forever, and Jesus alone on the throne.

Ruth Bell Graham

Jesus challenges you and me to keep our focus daily on the cross of His will if we want to be His disciples.

Anne Graham Lotz

For Further Reflection

Matthew 6:24; 10:38–39; Mark 8:34; Luke 9:23; John 13:15

Today's Prayer

Dear Lord, you sent Jesus to save the world and to save me. I thank you for Jesus, and I will do my best to follow him today and forever. Amen.

Too Friendly with the World?

Do not deceive yourselves. If any of you think you are wise by the standards of this age, you should become "fools" so that you may become wise. For the wisdom of this world is foolishness in God's sight. As it is written: "He catches the wise in their own craftiness."

1 Corinthians 3:18–19

We live in the world, but we should not worship it; yet at every turn, or so it seems, we are tempted to do otherwise. The world in which we live is a noisy, distracting place that offers countless temptations and dangers. The world seems to cry, "Worship me with your time, your money, your energy, your thoughts, and your life!" But if we are wise, we won't fall prey to that temptation.

If you wish to build your character day by day, you must distance yourself, at least in part, from the temptations and distractions of society. But distancing yourself isn't easy, especially when so many societal forces are struggling to capture your attention, your participation, and your money.

C. S. Lewis said, "Aim at heaven and you will get earth thrown in; aim at earth and you will get neither." Aim high . . . aim at heaven. When you do, you'll be strengthening your character as you improve every aspect of your life. And God will demonstrate his approval as he showers you with more spiritual blessings than you can count.

The world makes plenty of promises that it can't keep. God, on the other hand, keeps every single one of his promises. If you dwell on the world's messages, you're setting yourself up for disaster. If you dwell on God's message, you're setting yourself up for victory.

Christians don't fail to live as they should because they are in the world; they fail because the world has gotten into them.

Billy Graham

Our joy ends where love of the world begins.

C. H. Spurgeon

There is no hell on earth like horizontal living without God.

Charles Swindoll

For Further Reflection

Luke 9:25; 16:9–10; Titus 2:11–13;
1 Peter 2:11; 1 John 2:15–17

Today's Prayer

Dear Lord, give me wisdom and perspective. Guide me according to your plans for my life and according to your commandments. And keep me mindful, dear Lord, that your truth is—and will forever be—the ultimate truth. Amen.

Rebellion Invites Disaster

It is the Lord your God you must follow, and him you must revere. Keep his commands and obey him; serve him and hold fast to him.

Deuteronomy 13:4

For most of us, it is a daunting thought: one day, perhaps soon, we'll come face to face with our heavenly Father, and we'll be called to account for our actions here on Earth. Our personal histories will certainly not be surprising to God; he already knows everything about us. But the full scope of our activities may be surprising to us. Some of us will be pleasantly surprised; others will not be.

God's commandments are not offered as helpful hints or timely tips. God's commandments are not suggestions; they are ironclad rules for living–rules that we disobey at our own risk.

The English clergyman Thomas Fuller observed, "He does not believe who does not live according to his beliefs." These words are most certainly true. We may proclaim our beliefs to our heart's content, but our proclamations will mean nothing–to others or ourselves–unless we accompany our words with deeds that match.

Be honest with yourself as you consider ways that you have, in the last few days, disobeyed God. Then, think about specific ways that you can be more obedient today.

The Fall is simply and solely Disobedience—doing what you have been told not to do: and it results from Pride—from being too big for your boots, forgetting your place, thinking that you are God.

C. S. Lewis

Let us never suppose that obedience is impossible or that holiness is meant only for a select few. Our Shepherd leads us in paths of righteousness—not for our name's sake but for His.

Elisabeth Elliot

Only he who believes is obedient, and only he who is obedient believes.

Dietrich Bonhoeffer

For Further Reflection

1 Samuel 15:22; Acts 5:29;
1 Peter 1:13-15; 1 John 2:17; 3:24

Today's Prayer

Heavenly Father, when I turn my thoughts away from you and your Word, I suffer. But when I obey your commandments, when I place my faith in you, I am secure. Let me live according to your commandments. Direct my path far from the temptations and distractions of this world. And let me discover your will and follow it, dear Lord, this day and always. Amen.

Humility Strengthens Character

Therefore, as God's chosen people, holy and dearly loved, clothe yourselves with compassion, kindness, humility, gentleness and patience.

Colossians 3:12

We have heard these descriptive phrases on countless occasions: "He's a self-made man" or "She's a self-made woman." The truth is that none of us is self-made.

As Christians, we have a profound reason to be humble: we have been refashioned and saved by Jesus Christ, and that salvation came not because of our own good works but because of God's grace. Thus, we are not self-made, we are God-made and Christ-saved.

How, then, can we be boastful? The answer, of course, is that if we are honest with ourselves and with our God, we simply can't be boastful. We must, instead, be eternally grateful and exceedingly humble.

Humility is not, in most cases, a naturally occurring human trait. Most of us, it seems, are more than willing to stick out our chests and say, "Look at me; I did that!" But in our better moments, in the quiet moments when we search the depths of our own hearts, we know better. Whatever "that" great thing is, God did that, not us.

Remember that humility leads to happiness, and pride doesn't. Max Lucado writes, "God exalts humility. When God works in our lives, helping us to become humble, he gives us a permanent joy. Humility gives us a joy that cannot be taken away." Enough said.

Humility is not thinking less of yourself; it is thinking of yourself less.

RICK WARREN

The great characteristic of the saint is humility.

OSWALD CHAMBERS

If you know who you are in Christ, your personal ego is not an issue.

BETH MOORE

FOR FURTHER REFLECTION

2 Samuel 22:28; 2 Chronicles 7:14;
2 Corinthians 12:9; Ephesians 4:2; 1 Peter 5:5–7

Today's Prayer

Heavenly Father, Jesus clothed himself with humility when he chose to leave heaven and come to Earth to live and die for us, his children. Christ is my Master and my example. Clothe me with humility, Lord, so that I might be more like your Son, and keep me mindful that you are the giver and sustainer of life. To you, dear Lord, goes the glory and the praise. Amen.

Embracing God's Love

Unfailing love surrounds the one who trusts in him.

Psalm 32:10

When you chose to follow Jesus, God gave you a gift that is more precious than gold: the gift of eternal life. Now, what will you do in response to God's love?

- Will you ignore it or embrace it?
- Will you return it or neglect it?
- Will you receive it and share it . . . or not?

The answer to these simple questions will determine the level of your faith and the quality of your life.

When you form the habit of embracing God's love day in and day out, you feel differently about yourself, your neighbors, and your world. When you embrace God's love, you share his message and you obey his commandments.

When you accept the Father's gift of grace, you are blessed here on Earth and throughout all eternity. So do yourself a favor right now: accept God's love with open arms and welcome his Son, Jesus, into your heart.

God's heart is overflowing with love for you and yours. Accept that love. Return that love. Respect that love. And share that love. Today.

God's love is our greatest security blanket. Kay Arthur advises, "Snuggle in God's arms. When you are hurting, when you feel lonely or left out, let Him cradle you, comfort you, reassure you of His all-sufficient power and love." Enough said.

If you have an obedience problem, you have a love problem. Focus your attention on God's love.

Henry Blackaby

Even when we cannot see the why and wherefore of God's dealings, we know that there is love in and behind them, so we can rejoice always.

J. I. Packer

The life of faith is a daily exploration of the constant and countless ways in which God's grace and love are experienced.

Eugene Peterson

For Further Reflection

Song of Songs 2:4; Lamentations 3:22;
John 3:16; 15:9; 1 John 4:16

Today's Prayer

Thank you, dear God, for your love. You are my loving Father. I thank you for your love and for your Son. I will praise you, I will worship you, and, I will love you today, tomorrow, and forever. Amen.

With Wisdom Comes Character

Who is wise and understanding among you?
Let them show it by their good life, by deeds
done in the humility that comes from wisdom.

James 3:13

Sometimes, amid the demands of daily life, you will lose perspective. Life may seem out of balance, and the pressures of everyday living may seem overwhelming. What's needed is a fresh perspective, a restored sense of balance . . . and God's wisdom. If you call upon the Lord and seek to see the world through his eyes, he will give you guidance, wisdom, and perspective. When you make God's priorities your priorities, he will lead you according to his plan and according to his commandments. When you study God's teachings, you are reminded that God's reality is the ultimate reality.

Do you seek to live a life of righteousness and wisdom? If so:

- You must study the ultimate source of wisdom, the Word of God.
- You must seek out worthy mentors and listen carefully to their advice.
- You must associate, day in and day out, with godly men and women.

Then, as you accumulate wisdom, you must not keep it for yourself; you must, instead, share it with your friends and family members.

But be forewarned: if you sincerely seek to share your hard-earned wisdom with others, your actions must reflect the values that you hold dear. The best way to share your wisdom—perhaps the only way—is not by your words but by your example.

Need wisdom? God's got it. If you want it, then study God's Word and associate with godly people.

The more wisdom enters our hearts, the more we will be able to trust our hearts in difficult situations.

JOHN ELDREDGE

Wisdom is knowledge applied. Head knowledge is useless on the battlefield. Knowledge stamped on the heart makes one wise.

BETH MOORE

If you lack knowledge, go to school. If you lack wisdom, get on your knees.

VANCE HAVNER

For Further Reflection

Psalms 90:12; 111:10; Proverbs 1:5;
Matthew 7:24–25; James 1:5

Today's Prayer

Dear Lord, give me wisdom to love my family, to care for them, and to help them understand the wisdom of your Holy Word. Let me share your wisdom by the words I speak and the example that I set today and every day that I live. Amen.

DAY 66

Asserting Yourself, Protecting Your Character

The Spirit God gave us does not make us timid, but gives us power, love and self-discipline.

2 TIMOTHY 1:7

When Paul wrote to Timothy, he reminded his young protégé that the God he served was a bold God and that God's spirit empowered his children with boldness also. Like Timothy, we, too, face times of uncertainty and fear in the ever-changing world in which we live. God's message is the same to us today as it was to Timothy: we can live boldly because the spirit of God resides in us.

When your peers encourage you to do things that you know are wrong, are you bold enough to say no? Hopefully so. But if you haven't quite learned the fine art of assertiveness, don't feel like the Lone Ranger. Plenty of people, even people who are old enough to know better, still have trouble standing up for themselves.

If you really want to strengthen your character, you have no alternative: you must acquire assertiveness skills. Simply put, assertiveness is an essential component of a strong character. With assertiveness, you can stand on your own two feet; without it, you are doomed to follow the crowd wherever they may choose to go (and oftentimes, they choose to go in the wrong direction).

You're almost never too old to learn how to become more assertive. So do yourself this major-league favor: learn to say no politely, firmly, and often. When you do, you'll be protecting yourself and your character.

Today, ask yourself if you're being assertive enough at work, at home, or in between. Today, create a positive attitude by focusing on opportunities, not roadblocks.

Perhaps I am stronger than I think.

Thomas Merton

Jesus Christ's teaching never beats about the bush.

Oswald Chambers

God would rather have a man on the wrong side of the fence than on the fence. The worst enemies of apostles are not the opposers but the appeasers.

Vance Havner

For Further Reflection

Psalm 139:13–14; Proverbs 19:8; 20:5;
Romans 12:3; Hebrews 13:6

Today's Prayer

Lord, I have so much to learn and so many ways to improve myself, but you love me just as I am. Thank you for your love and for your Son. And help me to become the person that you want me to become. Amen.

Christ-Centered Leadership

Those who are wise will shine like the brightness of the heavens, and those who lead many to righteousness, like the stars for ever and ever.

Daniel 12:3

The old saying is familiar and true: Imitation is the sincerest form of flattery. As believers, we are called to imitate, as best we can, the carpenter from Galilee. The task of imitating Christ is often difficult and sometimes impossible, but as Christians, we must continually try.

Our world needs leaders who willingly honor Christ with their words and their deeds. If you seek to be such a leader, then you must begin by making yourself a worthy example to your family, to your friends, to your church, and to your community. After all, your words of instruction will never ring true unless you yourself are willing to follow them.

Christ-centered leadership is an exercise in service—service to God in heaven and service to his children here on Earth. Christ willingly became a servant to his followers, and you must seek to do the same for yours.

Are you the kind of servant-leader whom you would want to follow? If so, congratulations: you are honoring your Savior by imitating him. And that, of course, is the sincerest form of flattery.

In thinking about your leadership style, ask yourself this: "Who's my model?" If you're wise, you'll try, as best you can, to emulate Jesus.

The goal of leadership is to empower the whole people of God to discern and to discharge the Lord's will.

STANLEY GRENZ

The great illusion of leadership is to think that others can be led out of the desert by someone who has never been there.

HENRI NOUWEN

A true and safe leader is likely to be one who has not desire to lead, but is forced into a position of leadership by inward pressure of the Holy Spirit and the press of external situation.

A. W. TOZER

FOR FURTHER REFLECTION

Proverbs 16:13; Isaiah 32:8; John 13:13–17;
1 Timothy 3:2–3; 1 Peter 5:2

Today's Prayer

Heavenly Father, when I find myself in a position of leadership, let me follow your teachings and obey your commandments. Make me a person of integrity and wisdom, Lord, and make me a worthy example to those whom I serve. And let me turn to you, Lord, for guidance and for strength in all that I say and do. Amen.

Keeping a Proper Perspective

Now, brothers and sisters, I have applied these things to myself and Apollos for your benefit, so that you may learn from us the meaning of the saying, "Do not go beyond what is written." Then you will not be puffed up in being a follower of one of us over against the other.

1 Corinthians 4:6

For most of us, life is busy and complicated. Amid the rush and crush of the daily grind, it is easy to lose perspective . . . easy but wrong. When the world seems to be spinning out of control, we can regain perspective by slowing ourselves down and then turning our thoughts and prayers toward God.

Do you carve out quiet moments each day to offer thanksgiving and praise to your Creator? You should. During these moments of stillness, you will often sense the love and wisdom of our Lord.

Today and every day, make time to be still before God. When you do, you can face the day's complications with the wisdom, the perspective, and the power that only he can provide.

Keep life in perspective. Remember that your life is an integral part of God's grand plan. So don't become unduly upset over the minor inconveniences of life, and don't worry too much about today's setbacks—they're temporary.

Instead of being frustrated and overwhelmed by all that is going on in our world, go to the Lord and ask Him to give you His eternal perspective.

Kay Arthur

Joy is the direct result of having God's perspective on our daily lives and the effect of loving our Lord enough to obey His commands and trust His promises.

Bill Bright

Earthly fears are no fears at all. Answer the big question of eternity, and the little questions of life fall into perspective.

Max Lucado

For Further Reflection

Exodus 14:14; Psalms 4:4; 37:37; 46:10; 62:5

Today's Prayer

Dear Lord, when the pace of my life becomes frantic, slow me down and give me perspective. Give me the wisdom to realize that the problems of today are only temporary but that your love is eternal. When I become discouraged, keep me steady and sure so that I might do your will here on Earth and then live with you forever in heaven. Amen.

Getting to Know God Builds Character

I keep asking that the God of our Lord Jesus Christ, the glorious Father, may give you the Spirit of wisdom and revelation, so that you may know him better.

Ephesians 1:17

If you'd like to strengthen your character, try spending more time really getting to know God. How can you do it? Through worship, praise, Bible study, prayer, and silent meditation.

Do you ever wonder if God:

- Hears your prayers?
- Understands your feelings?
- Really knows your heart?

When you have doubts about your Father in heaven, remember this: God is right here, right now, listening to your thoughts and prayers, watching over your every move.

The Bible teaches that a wonderful way to get to know God is simply to be still and listen to him. But sometimes, you may find it hard to slow yourself down long enough to quiet your mind and tune up your heart. And as the demands of everyday life weigh down upon you, you may be tempted to ignore God's presence or—worse yet—to rebel against his commandments. But when you quiet yourself and acknowledge his presence, God touches your heart and restores your spirits. So why not let him do it right now? If you really want to know him better, silence is a wonderful place to start.

If you'd like to get to know God a little better, talk to him more often. The more often you speak to him, the more often he'll speak to you.

We can seek God and find him! God is knowable, touchable, hearable, seeable, with the mind, the hands, the ears, and eyes of the inner man.

A. W. TOZER

Christians have spent their whole lives mastering all sorts of principles, done their duty, carried on the programs of their church . . . and never known God intimately, heart to heart.

JOHN ELDREDGE

Here is our opportunity: we cannot see God, but we can see Christ. Christ was not only the Son of God, but He was the Father. Whatever Christ was, that God is.

HANNAH WHITALL SMITH

For Further Reflection

John 17:3; Galatians 4:8–9; Colossians 1:9–10; 2 Peter 1:5–6; 1 John 4:8

Today's Prayer

Dear Lord, help me remember the importance of silence. Help me discover quiet moments throughout the day so that I can sense your presence and your love. Amen.

The Right Places. The Right Friends

Walk with the wise and become wise, for a companion of fools suffers harm.

Proverbs 13:20

Whom will you try to please today: God or man? Your primary obligation, of course, is to please your Father in heaven. But you may, from time to time, feel the urge to impress your peers—and sometimes that urge can be strong.

Peer pressure can be a good thing or a bad thing, depending upon your peers. If your peers encourage you to follow God's will and to obey his commandments, then you'll experience positive peer pressure, and that's good. But if you are involved with friends who encourage you to do foolish things, you're facing a different kind of peer pressure . . . and you'd better beware. When you feel pressured to do things—or to say things—that lead you away from God, you're aiming straight for trouble. So don't do the easy thing or the popular thing. Do the right thing, and don't worry about winning popularity contests.

Rick Warren correctly observed, "Those who follow the crowd usually get lost in it." Are you satisfied to follow that crowd? If so, you will probably pay a heavy price for your shortsightedness. But if you're determined to follow the One from Galilee, he will guide your steps and bless your undertakings.

To sum it up, here's your choice: you can choose to please God first (and by doing so, strengthen your character), or you can fall prey to peer pressure. The choice is yours—and so are the consequences.

When you're torn between trusting your peers or trusting your conscience, trust your conscience.

You will get untold flak for prioritizing God's revealed and present will for your life over man's . . . but, boy, is it worth it.

BETH MOORE

Do you want to be wise? Choose wise friends.

CHARLES SWINDOLL

There is nothing that makes more cowards and feeble men than public opinion.

HENRY WARD BEECHER

FOR FURTHER REFLECTION

Proverbs 1:10; Acts 5:29; 1 Corinthians 15:33; 2 Corinthians 6:14; 3 John 1:11

Today's Prayer

Dear Lord, other people may encourage me to stray from your path, but I wish to follow in the footsteps of your Son. Give me the vision to see the right path—and the wisdom to follow it—today and every day of my life. Amen.

Matching Your Actions to Your Beliefs

Do not merely listen to the word, and so deceive yourselves. Do what it says.

James 1:22

It takes courage to stand up for our beliefs, but it takes character to live by them. Yet far too many of us spend more energy verbalizing our beliefs than living by them—with predictable consequences.

- Is your life a picture book of your beliefs?
- Are your actions congruent with your personal code?
- Are you willing to practice the philosophy that you preach?

If so, your character will take care of itself.

But if you're doing things that don't meet with the approval of the person you see in the mirror, it's time to slow down, step back, and think about how your conduct is shaping your character. If you profess to be a Christian but behave as if you were not, you're living in denial. And denial, in large doses, corrodes character.

So today, make certain that your actions are guided by God's Word and by the conscience that he has placed in your heart. Don't treat your faith as if it were separate from everyday life—instead, weave your beliefs into the very fabric of your day. When you do, God will honor your good works, and your good works will honor God.

Think about the importance of making your actions conform to your beliefs. Then, ask yourself if your behavior matches your rhetoric. If the answer is yes, congratulations. If not, think of a single step you can take today to stand up for the things you believe in.

Believe and do what God says. The life-changing consequences will be limitless, and the results will be confidence and peace of mind.

Franklin Graham

God delights to meet the faith of one who looks up to Him and says, "Lord, You know that I cannot do this–but I believe that You can!"

Amy Carmichael

Jesus taught that the evidence that confirms our leaps of faith comes after we risk believing, not before.

Gloria Gaither

For Further Reflection

Matthew 8:13; Mark 9:23; John 20:27;
2 Timothy 1:12; 1 John 5:1

Today's Prayer

Heavenly Father, I believe in you, and I believe in your Word. Help me to live in such a way that my actions validate my beliefs–and let the glory be yours forever. Amen.

Walk in God's Truth

Teach me your way, O Lord,
that I may rely on your faithfulness.

Psalm 86:11

A righteous life has many components. To name but a few:

- Faith
- Honesty
- Generosity
- Love
- Kindness
- Humility
- Gratitude
- Worship

If we seek to follow the steps of our Savior, Jesus Christ, we must seek to live according to his commandments.

When we seek righteousness in our own lives–and when we seek the companionship of like-minded friends–we not only build our characters, but we also reap the spiritual rewards that God offers those who obey him. When we live in accordance with God's commandments, he blesses us in ways that we cannot fully understand.

Are you ready, willing, able, and anxious to receive God's blessings? Then obey him. And rest assured that when you do your part, he'll do his part.

God has given us his commandments for a reason: to obey them. These commandments are not suggestions, helpful hints, or friendly reminders–they are rules we must live by . . . or else!

The Ten Commandments were given to evoke fear and reverence for the Holy One so that obedience and blessing might result.

BETH MOORE

Let us remember therefore this lesson: That to worship our God sincerely we must evermore begin by hearkening to His voice, and by giving ear to what He commands us. For if every man goes after his own way, we shall wander. We may well run, but we shall never be a whit nearer to the right way, but rather farther away from it.

JOHN CALVIN

Bible history is filled with people who began the race with great success but failed at the end because they disregarded God's rules.

WARREN WIERSBE

For Further Reflection

Psalm 112:1; Proverbs 13:13; Ecclesiastes 5:1; John 14:21-23; 1 John 5:3

Today's Prayer

Thank you, dear Lord, for loving me enough to give me rules to live by. Let me live by your commandments, and let me lead others to do the same. Let me walk righteously in your way, dear Lord, this day and every day. Amen.

Critics Beware

Brothers and sisters, do not slander one another. Anyone who speaks against a brother or sister or judges them speaks against the law and judges it. When you judge the law, you are not keeping it, but sitting in judgment on it.

James 4:11

From experience, we know that it is easier to criticize than to correct; we understand that it is easier to find faults than solutions; and we realize that excessive criticism is usually destructive, not productive. Yet the urge to criticize others remains a powerful temptation for most of us. Our task, as obedient believers, is to break the twin habits of negative thinking and critical speech.

In the book of James, we are issued a clear warning: "Brothers and sisters, do not slander one another" (4:11). Undoubtedly, James understood the paralyzing power of chronic negativity, and so must we. Negativity is highly contagious: we give it to others who, in turn, give it back to us. Thankfully, this cycle can be broken by positive thoughts, heartfelt prayers, and encouraging words.

As you examine the quality of your own communications, can you honestly say that you're a booster not a critic? If so, keep up the good words. But if you're occasionally overwhelmed by negativity and if you pass that negativity along to your neighbors, it's time for a mental housecleaning.

As a thoughtful Christian, you can use the transforming power of Christ's love to break the chains of negativity. And you should.

Negative thinking breeds more negative thinking, so nip negativity in the bud, starting today and continuing every day of your life.

We shall never come to the perfect man, till we come to the perfect world.

MATTHEW HENRY

Being critical of others, including God, is one way we try to avoid facing and judging our own sins.

WARREN WIERSBE

Positive anything is better than negative nothing.

ELBERT HUBBARD

For Further Reflection

Proverbs 15:1; Matthew 7:1–5; Luke 6:37–42; Romans 14:1–4; James 5:9

Today's Prayer

Thank you, Lord, for your infinite love. Make me an optimistic Christian, Father, as I place my hope and my trust in you. Amen.

The Spiritual Journey

Grow in the grace and knowledge of our Lord and Savior Jesus Christ. To him be glory both now and forever! Amen.

2 Peter 3:18

When it comes to your faith, God doesn't intend for you to stand still. He wants you to keep moving and growing. In fact, God's plan for you includes a lifetime of prayer, praise, and spiritual growth.

Many of life's most important lessons are painful to learn. During times of heartbreak and hardship, we must be courageous and we must be patient, knowing that in his own time, God will heal us, if we invite him into our hearts.

Spiritual growth need not take place only in times of adversity. We must seek to grow in our knowledge and love of the Lord every day that we live. In those quiet moments when we open our hearts to God, the One who made us keeps remaking us. He gives us direction, perspective, wisdom, and courage. The appropriate moment to accept those spiritual gifts is the present one.

Are you as mature as you're ever going to be? Hopefully not! When it comes to your faith, God doesn't intend for you to become "fully grown," at least not in this lifetime. In fact, God still has important lessons that he intends to teach you. So ask yourself this: "What lesson is God trying to teach me today?" And then go about the business of learning it.

There is wonderful freedom and joy in coming to recognize that the fun is in the becoming.

GLORIA GAITHER

Our heavenly Father knows to place us where we may learn lessons impossible anywhere else. He has neither misplaced nor displaced us.

ELISABETH ELLIOT

The whole idea of belonging to Christ is to look less and less like we used to and more and more like Him.

ANGELA THOMAS

For Further Reflection

Psalm 66:10-12; Ephesians 3:19; Colossians 1:9; Hebrews 6:1; 2 Timothy 2:22

Today's Prayer

Dear Lord, the Bible tells me that you are at work in my life, continuing to help me grow and to mature in my faith. Show me your wisdom, Father, and let me live according to your Word and your will. Amen.

Beyond Failure

Success, success to you, and success to those who help you, for your God will help you.

1 Chronicles 12:18

Life's occasional setbacks are simply the price that we must pay for taking risks and following our dreams. But even when we encounter bitter disappointments, we must never lose faith.

Hebrews 10:36 advises, "Persevere so that when you have done the will of God, you will receive what he has promised." These words remind us that when we persevere, we will eventually receive the rewards that God has promised us. What's required is perseverance, not perfection.

When we face hardships, God stands ready to protect us. Our responsibility, of course, is to ask him for protection. When we call upon him in heartfelt prayer, he will answer—in his own time and according to his own plan—and he will do his part to heal us. We, of course, must do our part, too.

And while we are waiting for God's plans to unfold and for his healing touch to restore us, we can be comforted in the knowledge that our Creator can overcome any obstacle, even if we cannot.

Remember that failure isn't permanent . . . unless you fail to get up. So pick yourself up, dust yourself off, and trust God. He will make it right. Warren Wiersbe had this advice: "No matter how badly we have failed, we can always get up and begin again. Our God is the God of new beginnings." And don't forget: the best time to begin again is now.

Do not be one of those who, rather than risk failure, never attempt anything.

Thomas Merton

To have failed is to own more wisdom, understanding, and experience than do those who sit on life's sidelines playing it safe.

Susan Lenzkes

One of the ways God refills us after failure is through the blessing of Christian fellowship. Just experiencing the joy of simple activities shared with other children of God can have a healing effect on us.

Anne Graham Lotz

For Further Reflection

Psalm 40:1–3; Proverbs 15:31; 28:13;
2 Corinthians 4:16; 1 John 1:9

Today's Prayer

Dear Lord, when I encounter failures and disappointments, keep me mindful that you are in control. Let me persevere—even if my soul is troubled—and let me follow your Son, Jesus Christ, this day and forever. Amen.

Subtle Immorality

Everyone who does evil hates the light, and will not come into the light for fear that their deeds will be exposed. But whoever lives by the truth comes into the light, so that it may be seen plainly that what they have done has been done in the sight of God.

John 3:20–21

Sin tears down character. When we yield to the distractions and temptations of this troubled world, we suffer. But God has other intentions, and his plans for our lives do not include sin or denial.

As creatures of free will, we may disobey God whenever we choose, but when we do so, we put ourselves and our loved ones in peril. Why?

- We cannot sin against God without consequence.
- We cannot live outside his will without injury.
- We cannot distance ourselves from God without hardening our hearts.
- We cannot yield to the ever-tempting distractions of our world and, at the same time, enjoy God's peace.

Sometimes, in a futile attempt to justify our behaviors, we make a distinction between "big" sins and "little" ones. To do so is a mistake. Sins of all shapes and sizes have the power to do us great harm. And in a world where sin is big business, that's certainly a sobering thought.

Sometimes immorality is obvious and sometimes it's not. So beware: the most subtle forms of sin are the most dangerous.

Man prefers to believe what he prefers to be true.

FRANCIS BACON

There's none so blind as those who will not see.

MATTHEW HENRY

Abide in Jesus, the sinless one—which means, give up all of self and its life, and dwell in God's will and rest in His strength. This is what brings the power that does not commit sin.

ANDREW MURRAY

FOR FURTHER REFLECTION

Romans 3:23; Hebrews 12:1;
1 John 1:8–9; 3:4; 2 John 1:9

Today's Prayer

Dear Lord, when I displease you, I do injury to myself, to my family, and to my community. Because sin distances me from you, Lord, I will fear sin and I will avoid sinful places. The fear of sinning against you is a healthy fear, Father, because it can motivate me to accomplish your will. Let a healthy fear of sin guide my path today and every day of my life. Amen.

God Is Sufficient

He said to me, "My grace is sufficient for you, for my power is made perfect in weakness."

2 CORINTHIANS 12:9

Of this you can be certain: God is sufficient to meet your needs. Period.

Do the demands of life seem overwhelming at times? If so, you must learn to rely, not only upon your own resources, but also upon the promises of your Father in heaven. God will hold your hand and walk with you and your family, if you let him. So even if your circumstances are difficult, trust the Father.

The psalmist writes, "Weeping may stay for a night, but rejoicing comes in the morning" (Psalm 30:5). But when we are suffering, the morning may seem very far away. It is not. God promises that he "is close to the brokenhearted" (Psalm 34:18). When we are troubled, we must turn to him, and we must encourage our friends and family members to do likewise.

If you are discouraged by the inevitable demands of life, be mindful of this fact: the loving heart of God is sufficient to meet any challenge . . . including yours.

If you'd like infinite protection, there's only one place you can receive it: from an infinite God. So remember: when you live in the center of God's will, you will also be living in the center of God's protection.

I grew up learning to be self-reliant, but now, to grow up in Christ, I must unlearn self-reliance and learn self-distrust in light of his all-sufficiency.

Mary Morrison Suggs

God's saints in all ages have realized that God was enough for them. God is enough for time; God is enough for eternity. God is enough!

Hannah Whitall Smith

God is always sufficient in perfect proportion to our need.

Beth Moore

For Further Reflection

1 Corinthians 15:10; 2 Corinthians 3:5; 12:9; Philippians 4:19; 2 Peter 1:3

Today's Prayer

Dear Lord, as I face the challenges of this day, you protect me. I thank you, Father, for your love and for your strength. I will lean upon you today and forever. Amen.

Controlling Your Temper

My dear brothers and sisters, take note of this: Everyone should be quick to listen, slow to speak and slow to become angry, because human anger does not produce the righteousness that God desires.

James 1:19–20

Anger often leads to impulsivity; impulsivity often leads to poor decision-making; and poor decision-making tends to tear down character. So if you'd like to increase your storehouse of wisdom while, at the same time, strengthen your character, you should learn to control your temper before your temper controls you.

When you allow yourself to become angry, you are certain to defeat at least one person: yourself. When you allow the minor frustrations of everyday life to hijack your emotions, you do harm to yourself and to your loved ones. So today and every day, guard yourself against the kind of angry thinking that inevitably takes a toll on your emotions and your relationships.

Don't allow feelings of anger or frustration to rule your life or, for that matter, your day. Your life is simply too short for that, and you deserve much better treatment than that.

If you think you're about to explode in anger, don't! Instead of striking back at someone, it's better to slow down, catch your breath, consider your options, and walk away if you must. Striking out in anger can lead to big problems. So it's better to walk away—and keep walking—than to blurt out angry words that can't be taken back.

Bitterness and anger, usually over trivial things, make havoc of homes, churches, and friendships.

Warren Wiersbe

From what does such contrariness arise in habitually angry people, but from a secret cause of too high an opinion of themselves so that it pierces their hearts when they see any man esteem them less than they esteem themselves? An inflated estimation of ourselves is more than half the weight of our wrath.

St. Thomas More

No one can heal himself by wounding someone else.

St. Ambrose

For Further Reflection

Proverbs 15:1; 29:11; 30:33;
Ephesians 4:26; James 1:20

Today's Prayer

Lord, when I become angry, help me to remember that you offer me peace. Let me turn to you for wisdom, for patience, and for the peace that only you can give. Amen.

Making Peace with the Past

Forget the former things; do not dwell on the past. See, I am doing a new thing! Now it springs up; do you not perceive it? I am making a way in the wilderness and streams in the wasteland.

Isaiah 43:18–19

One of the things that fits nicely into the category of "things we cannot change" is the past. Yet even though we know that the past is unchangeable, many of us continue to invest energy worrying about the unfairness of yesterday (when we should, instead, be focusing on the opportunities of today and the promises of tomorrow).

Author Hannah Whitall Smith observed, "How changed our lives would be if we could only fly through the days on wings of surrender and trust!" These words remind us that even when we cannot understand the past, we must trust God and accept his will.

So if you've endured a difficult past, accept it and learn from it, but don't spend too much time here in the precious present fretting over memories of the unchangeable past. Instead, trust God's plan and look to the future. After all, the future is where everything that's going to happen to you from this moment on is going to take place.

The past is past, so don't live there. If you're focused on the past, change your focus. If you're living in the past, it's time to stop living there, starting now.

Shake the dust from your past, and move forward in His promises.

KAY ARTHUR

Whoever you are, whatever your condition or circumstance, whatever your past or problem, Jesus can restore you to wholeness.

ANNE GRAHAM LOTZ

Yesterday is just experience but tomorrow is glistening with purpose—and today is the channel leading from one to the other.

BARBARA JOHNSON

FOR FURTHER REFLECTION

Galatians 2:20–22; Philippians 3:13–14;
2 Corinthians 5:17–18

Today's Prayer

Heavenly Father, free me from anger, resentment, and envy. When I am bitter, I cannot feel the peace that you intend for my life. Keep me mindful that forgiveness is your commandment, and help me accept the past, treasure the present, and trust the future to you. Amen.

Problem-Solving Builds Character

The righteous person may have many troubles,
but the LORD delivers him from them all.

PSALM 34:19

Life is an adventure in problem-solving. The question is not whether we will encounter problems; the real question is how we will choose to address them. When it comes to solving the problems of everyday living, we often know precisely what needs to be done, but we may be slow in doing it—especially if what needs to be done is difficult. So we put off till tomorrow what should be done today.

As a person living in the twenty-first century, you have your own set of challenges. As you face those challenges, be comforted by this fact: troubles—of every kind—are temporary. Yet God's grace is eternal. And worries—of every kind—are temporary. But God's love is everlasting. The troubles that concern you will pass. God remains. And for every problem, God has a solution.

The words of Psalm 34 remind us that the Lord solves problems for "the righteous person." And usually, doing what is right means doing the uncomfortable work of confronting our problems sooner rather than later. So let the problem-solving begin—right now.

Today, think about the wisdom of tackling your problems sooner rather than later. Remember that "this too will pass," but whatever "it" is will pass more quickly if you spend more time solving your problems and less time fretting about them.

We are all faced with a series of great opportunities, brilliantly disguised as unsolvable problems. Unsolvable without God's wisdom, that is.

Charles Swindoll

Life will be made or broken at the place where we meet and deal with obstacles.

E. Stanley Jones

God has plans–not problems–for our lives. Before she died in the concentration camp in Ravensbruck, my sister Betsie said to me, "Corrie, your whole life has been a training for the work you are doing here in prison–and for the work you will do afterward."

Corrie ten Boom

For Further Reflection

Psalm 50:15; Proverbs 3:5-6; Matthew 7:7; Philippians 4:6-7, 13

Today's Prayer

Lord, sometimes my problems are simply too big for me, but they are never too big for you. Let me turn my troubles over to you, Lord, and let me trust in you today and for all eternity. Amen.

Discipleship Builds Character

He has shown you, O mortal, what is good. And what does the LORD require of you? To act justly and to love mercy and to walk humbly with your God.

MICAH 6:8

When Jesus addressed his disciples, he warned that each one must "take up their cross and follow me" (Matthew 16:24). The disciples must have known exactly what the Master meant. In Jesus' day, prisoners were forced to carry their own crosses to the location where they would be put to death. Thus, Christ's message was clear: in order to follow him, Christ's disciples must deny themselves and, instead, trust him completely. Nothing has changed since then.

If we are to be disciples of Christ, we must trust him and place him at the very center of our beings. Jesus never comes next. He is always first. The paradox, of course, is that only by sacrificing ourselves to him do we gain salvation for ourselves.

The nineteenth-century writer Hannah Whitall Smith observed, "The crucial question for each of us is this: What do you think of Jesus, and do you yet have a personal acquaintance with him?" Indeed, the answer to that question will determine the quality, the course, and the direction of your life today and for all eternity.

Jesus has called upon believers of every generation (and that includes you) to walk with him. Jesus promises that when you follow in his footsteps, he will teach you how to live freely and lightly (Matthew 11:28–30). And when Jesus makes a promise, you can depend upon it.

Today, think of at least one single step that you can take to become a better disciple for Christ. Then, take that step.

A life lived in God is not lived on the plane of feelings, but of the will.

ELISABETH ELLIOT

If we just give God the little that we have, we can trust Him to make it go around.

GLORIA GAITHER

A disciple is a follower of Christ. That means you take on His priorities as your own. His agenda becomes your agenda. His mission becomes your mission.

CHARLES STANLEY

FOR FURTHER REFLECTION

Matthew 16:24; Ephesians 5:1; 6:6–7; 2 Thessalonians 1:11–12; 1 John 3:3

Today's Prayer

Help me, Lord, to understand what cross I am to bear this day. Give me the strength and the courage to carry that cross along the path of your choosing so that I may be a worthy disciple of your Son. Amen.

Building Character in Silence

Be still before the LORD and wait patiently for him.

PSALM 37:7

Here's a simple little prescription for character building: carve out a little time for silence every day.

Here in our noisy, twenty-first-century world, silence is highly underrated. Many of us can't even seem to walk from the front door to the street without a cell phone in our ear. The world seems to grow louder day by day, and our senses seem to be invaded at every turn. But if we allow the distractions of a clamorous society to separate us from God's peace, we do ourselves a profound disservice. So if we're wise, we make time each day for quiet reflection. And when we do, we are rewarded.

Do you take time each day for an extended period of silence? And during those precious moments, do you sincerely open your heart to your Creator? If so, you will be blessed. If not, then the struggles and stresses of everyday living may rob you of the peace that should rightfully be yours because of your personal relationship with Christ. So take time each day to quietly commune with your Savior.

Want to talk to God? Then don't make him shout. If you really want to hear from God, go to a quiet place and listen. If you keep listening long enough and carefully enough, he'll start talking.

Silence is as fit a garment for devotion as any other language.

C. H. Spurgeon

Growth takes place in quietness, in hidden ways, in silence and solitude. The process is not accessible to observation.

Eugene Peterson

The Lord Jesus, available to people much of the time, left them, sometimes a great while before day, to go up to the hills where He could commune in solitude with His Father.

Elisabeth Elliot

For Further Reflection

Ecclesiastes 3:7; Proverbs 3:6–7; 16:20; 17:28; James 1:19

Today's Prayer

Dear Lord, in the quiet moments of this day, I will turn my thoughts and prayers to you. In silence I will sense your presence, and I will seek your will for my life, knowing that when I accept your peace, I will be blessed today and throughout eternity. Amen.

God Wants to Teach

Who, then, are those who fear the Lord? He will instruct them in the ways they should choose.

Psalm 25:12

The Bible promises that God will guide you if you let him. Your job, of course, is to let him. But sometimes, you will be tempted to do otherwise. Sometimes, you'll be tempted to go along with the crowd; other times, you'll be tempted to do things your way, not God's way. When you feel those temptations, you must resist them—or else.

What will you allow to guide you through the coming day: your own desires (or, for that matter, the desires of your peers)? Or will you allow God to lead the way? The answer should be obvious. You should let God be your guide. When you entrust your life to him completely and without reservation, God will give you the strength to meet any challenge, the courage to face any trial, and the wisdom to live in his righteousness. So trust him today and seek his guidance. When you do, your character will most certainly take care of itself, and your next step will most assuredly be the right one.

Would you like God's guidance? Then ask him for it. When you pray for guidance, God will give it (Luke 11:9). So ask.

Fix your eyes upon the Lord! Do it once. Do it daily. Do it constantly. Look at the Lord and keep looking at Him.

CHARLES SWINDOLL

We have ample evidence that the Lord is able to guide. The promises cover every imaginable situation. All we need to do is to take the hand he stretches out.

ELISABETH ELLIOT

We must always invite Jesus to be the navigator of our plans, desires, wills, and emotions, for He is the way, the truth, and the life.

BILL BRIGHT

For Further Reflection

Exodus 4:15; Isaiah 48:17; Isaiah 50:4-5; Jeremiah 32:33; 1 Thessalonians 4:9

Today's Prayer

Dear Lord, Thank you for your constant presence and your constant love. I draw near to you this day with the confidence that you are ready to guide me. Help me walk closely with you, Father, and help me share your Good News with all who cross my path. Amen.

Love Is a Choice

My command is this: Love each other as I have loved you. Greater love has no one than this: to lay down one's life for one's friends.

John 15:12–13

Love is a choice. Either you choose to behave lovingly toward others . . . or not; either you behave yourself in ways that enhance your relationships . . . or not. But make no mistake: genuine love requires effort. Simply put, if you wish to build lasting relationships, you must be willing to do your part.

Since the days of Adam and Eve, God has allowed his children to make choices for themselves, and so it is with you. As you interact with family and friends, you have choices to make . . . lots of them. If you choose wisely, you'll be rewarded; if you choose unwisely, you'll bear the consequences.

Christ's words are clear: we are to love God first, and second, we are to love others as we love ourselves (Matthew 22:37–40). These two commandments are seldom easy, and because we are imperfect beings, we often fall short. But God's Holy Word commands us to try.

The Christian path is an exercise in love and forgiveness. If we are to walk in Christ's footsteps, we must forgive those who have done us harm, and we must accept Christ's love by sharing it freely with family, friends, neighbors, and strangers.

Do you want love to last? Then you must understand this: genuine love requires effort. That's why those who are lazy in love are often losers in love, too!

No man truly has joy unless he lives in love.

THOMAS AQUINAS

Homes that are built on anything other than love are bound to crumble.

BILLY GRAHAM

Those who abandon ship the first time it enters a storm miss the calm beyond. And the rougher the storms weathered together, the deeper and stronger real love grows.

RUTH BELL GRAHAM

For Further Reflection

1 Corinthians 13:1; 1 Thessalonians 3:12;
1 Peter 1:22; 4:8; 1 John 4:11

Today's Prayer

Lord, you have given me the gift of love and you've asked me to share it. The gift of love is a precious gift indeed. Let me nurture love and treasure it. And help me remember that the essence of love is not to receive it but to give it today and forever. Amen.

Got Strength?

Create in me a pure heart, O God, and renew a steadfast spirit within me. Do not cast me from your presence or take your Holy Spirit from me. Restore to me the joy of your salvation and grant me a willing spirit, to sustain me.

PSALM 51:10–12

Today, like every other day, is literally brimming with possibilities. Whether we realize it or not, God is always working in us and through us; our job is to let him do his work without undue interference. Yet we are imperfect beings who, because of our limited vision, often resist God's will. And oftentimes, because of our stubborn insistence on squeezing too many activities into a twenty-four-hour day, we allow ourselves to become exhausted or frustrated—or both.

- Are you tired or troubled? Turn your heart toward God in prayer.
- Are you weak or worried? Make the time to delve deeply into God's Holy Word.
- Are you spiritually depleted? Call upon fellow believers to support you, and call upon Christ to renew your spirit and your life.
- Are you simply overwhelmed by the demands of the day? Pray for the wisdom to simplify your life.
- Are you exhausted? Pray for the wisdom to rest a little more and worry a little less.

When you do these things, you'll discover that the Creator of the universe stands always ready and always able to create a new sense of wonderment and joy in you.

Need strength? Let God's spirit reign over your heart. And remember that the best time to begin living triumphantly is the present moment.

The resurrection of Jesus Christ is the power of God to change history and to change lives.

Bill Bright

Cast yourself into the arms of God and be very sure that if He wants anything of you, He will fit you for the work and give you strength.

Philip Neri

No giant will ever be a match for a big God with a little rock.

Beth Moore

For Further Reflection

Joshua 1:9; Psalm 31:24; Isaiah 40:31; 41:10; 43:2

Today's Prayer

Dear Lord, sometimes the demands of the day leave me discouraged and frustrated. Renew my strength, Father, and give me patience and perspective. Today and every day, let me draw comfort and courage from your promises, from your love, and from your Son. Amen.

Observing the Sabbath

Remember the Sabbath day by keeping it holy.

Exodus 20:8

When God gave Moses the Ten Commandments, it became perfectly clear that our heavenly Father intended for us to make the Sabbath a holy day—a day for worship, for contemplation, for fellowship, and for rest. Yet we live in a seven-day-a-week world, a world that all too often treats Sunday as a regular workday.

One way to strengthen your character is by giving God at least one day each week. If you carve out the time for a day of worship and praise, you'll be amazed at the impact it will have on the rest of your week. But if you fail to honor God's day, if you treat the Sabbath as a day to work or a day to party, you'll miss out on a harvest of blessings that is only available one day each week.

How does your family observe the Lord's day? When church is over, do you treat Sunday like any other day of the week? If so, it's time to think long and hard about your family's schedule and your family's priorities. And if you've been treating Sunday as just another day, it's time to break that habit. When Sunday rolls around, don't try to fill every spare moment. Take time to rest . . . Father's orders!

Today, think about new ways that you can honor God on the Sabbath. The Sabbath is unlike the other six days of the week, and it's up to you to treat it that way.

Worship is not taught from the pulpit. It must be learned in the heart.

JIM ELLIOT

Worship is a daunting task. Each worships differently. But each should worship.

MAX LUCADO

God has promised to give you all of eternity. The least you can do is give Him one day a week in return.

MARIE T. FREEMAN

For Further Reflection

Genesis 2:3; Exodus 20:8–11; 1 Chronicles 23:31; Mark 2:27–28; Hebrews 4:9–11

Today's Prayer

Dear Lord, I thank you for the Sabbath, a day when my family and I can worship you and praise your Son. We will keep the Sabbath as a holy day, a day when we can honor you. Amen.

Staying Off the Slippery Slope

Jesus replied, "Very truly I tell you, everyone who sins is a slave to sin."

John 8:34

The temptations of the world sit atop a slippery slope. If you sample those temptations even once, you're on that slope. Perhaps, if you're lucky, you can keep your footing. Perhaps not. But of this you can be certain: if you never step foot on the slippery slope of sin, you'll never slide down.

You live in a world that encourages you to try any number of things that are dangerous to your spiritual, mental, and/or physical health. It's a world brimming with traps and temptations designed to corrupt your character, ruin your health, sabotage your relationships, and wreck your life. And by the way, you know precisely which temptations are most tempting to you and, therefore, the most dangerous.

Invariably, addictive substances and destructive behaviors are described, at least in the beginning, as harmless pleasures, but they're not. So your job, as a rational person and a well-meaning Christian, is to do the following: never experiment with an activity that you wouldn't want to become a full-blown habit. Why? Because when it comes to the temptations of this world, it's easier to stay out than to get out. In other words, the best time to cure a bad habit is before it starts.

When given the opportunity to try something that might turn into a bad habit, don't. The slippery slope might be steeper than it looks.

Faith in Christ is the victory that overcomes not only the world but also every engrained sin of the flesh.

JIM CYMBALA

As a child of God, you are no longer a slave to sin.

KAY ARTHUR

There is nothing wrong with asking God's direction. But it is wrong to go our own way, then expect Him to bail us out.

LARRY BURKETT

For Further Reflection

Mark 7:20–23; Romans 12:1–2; 1 Corinthians 10:13; 1 Timothy 6:10; James 4:7

Today's Prayer

Dear Lord, give me the wisdom and the strength to stay far away from the temptations of this world. Keep me mindful that there are no *little* sins and that the only lasting peace comes, not from the world, but from you. Amen.

Holding On to Hope

We have this hope as an anchor for the soul, firm and secure.

HEBREWS 6:19

In difficult times, hope can be elusive. But those who place their faith in God's promises need never lose hope. After all:

- God is good.
- God's love endures.
- God has promised his children the gift of eternal life.
- God keeps his promises.

Despite God's promises, despite Christ's love, and despite our countless blessings, we frail human beings can still lose hope from time to time. When we do, we need the encouragement of Christian friends, the life-changing power of prayer, and the healing truth of God's Holy Word.

If you find a friend in need, remind him or her of the peace that is found through a personal relationship with Christ. It was Christ who promised, "I have told you these things, so that in me you may have peace. In this world you will have trouble. But take heart! I have overcome the world" (John 16:33). This world can be a place of trials and tribulations, but as believers, we are secure. God has promised us peace, joy, and eternal life. And, of course, God keeps his promises today, tomorrow, and forever.

If you're experiencing hard times, you'll be wise to start spending more time with God. And if you do your part, God will do his part. So never be afraid to hope—or to ask—for a miracle.

Faith looks back and draws courage; hope looks ahead and keeps desire alive.

John Eldredge

The hope we have in Jesus is the anchor for the soul—something sure and steadfast, preventing drifting or giving way, lowered to the depth of God's love.

Franklin Graham

Love is the seed of all hope. It is the enticement to trust, to risk, to try, and to go on.

Gloria Gaither

For Further Reflection

Psalm 38:15; Lamentations 3:25–26;
Romans 15:13; Hebrews 10:23; 11:1

Today's Prayer

Today, dear Lord, I will live in hope. If I become discouraged, I will turn to you. If I grow weary, I will seek strength in you. In every aspect of my life, I will trust you. You are my Father, Lord, and I place my hope and faith in you. Amen.

The Right Kind of Fear

Better a little with the fear of the Lord
than great wealth with turmoil.

Proverbs 15:16

Do you possesses a healthy, fearful respect for God's power? Hopefully so. After all, the lesson from the book of Proverbs is clear: "The fear of the Lord is the beginning of knowledge, but fools despise wisdom and instruction" (1:7). To fear God is:

- To acknowledge his sovereignty over every aspect of his creation (including you)
- To place your relationship with God in its proper perspective—he is your master; you are his servant
- To dread the very thought of disobeying him
- To humble yourself in the presence of his infinite power and his infinite love

God's greatest servants will always be those humble men and women who care less for their own glory and more for God's glory. We must respect him and we must humbly obey his commandments, or we must accept the consequences of our misplaced pride. When we fear the Creator—and when we honor him by obeying his teachings—we receive God's approval and his blessings. But when we ignore him or disobey his commandments, we invite disastrous consequences.

The fear of the Lord is, indeed, the beginning of knowledge. So today, as you face the realities of everyday life, remember this: until you acquire a healthy, respectful fear of God's power, your education is incomplete, and so is your faith.

The remarkable thing about fearing God is that when you fear God, you fear nothing else, whereas if you do not fear God, you fear everything else.

OSWALD CHAMBERS

When true believers are awed by the greatness of God and by the privilege of becoming His children, then they become sincerely motivated, effective evangelists.

BILL HYBELS

A healthy fear of God will do much to deter us from sin.

CHARLES SWINDOLL

FOR FURTHER REFLECTION

Deuteronomy 6:24; Psalms 34:7; 112:1; 115:13; Proverbs 19:23

Today's Prayer

Lord, you love me and protect me. I praise you, Father, for your grace, and I respect you for your infinite power. Let my greatest fear in life be the fear of displeasing you. Amen.

Listen Carefully to God

Whoever belongs to God hears what God says.
The reason you do not hear is that you
do not belong to God.

JOHN 8:47

Sometimes God speaks loudly and clearly. More often, he speaks in a quiet voice—and if you are wise, you will be listening carefully when he does. To do so, you must carve out quiet moments each day to study his Word and sense his direction. And you can be sure that every time you listen to God, you receive a lesson in character building.

- Can you quiet yourself long enough to listen to your conscience?
- Are you attuned to the subtle guidance of your intuition?
- Are you willing to pray sincerely and then to wait quietly for God's response?

Hopefully so, because the more carefully you listen to your Creator, the more he will work in you and through you.

Usually God refrains from sending his messages on stone tablets. More often, he communicates in subtler ways. If you sincerely desire to hear his voice (and strengthen your character), you must listen carefully, and you must do so in the silent corners of your quiet, willing heart.

Today, take a few moments to consider the fact that prayer is two-way communication with God. Talking to God isn't enough; you should also listen to him.

In the soul-searching of our lives, we are to stay quiet so we can hear Him say all that He wants to say to us in our hearts.

Charles Swindoll

When we come to Jesus stripped of pretensions, with a needy spirit, ready to listen, He meets us at the point of need.

Catherine Marshall

Half an hour of listening is essential except when one is very busy. Then, a full hour is needed.

St. Francis de Sales

For Further Reflection

Matthew 7:24; Luke 6:46; John 10:27–28; Romans 10:17; Hebrews 4:12; 2 Timothy 3:16

Today's Prayer

Lord, give me the wisdom to be a good listener. Help me listen carefully to my family, to my friends, and—most importantly—to you. Amen.

Real Repentance Builds Character

Whoever conceals their sins does not prosper, but the one who confesses and renounces them finds mercy.

Proverbs 28:13

Who among us has sinned? All of us. But God calls upon us to turn away from sin by following his commandments. The good news: when we ask God's forgiveness and turn our hearts to him, he forgives us absolutely and completely.

Genuine repentance requires more than simply offering God apologies for our misdeeds. Real repentance may start with feelings of sorrow and remorse, but it ends only when we turn away from the sin that has heretofore distanced us from our Creator. In truth, we offer our most meaningful apologies to God, not with our words, but with our actions. As long as we are still engaged in sin, we may be *repenting*, but we have not fully *repented*.

Is there an aspect of your life that is distancing you from your God? If so, ask for his forgiveness—and just as importantly, stop sinning. Then, wrap yourself in the protection of God's Word. When you do, both you and your character will be secure.

If you're engaged in behavior that is displeasing to God, today is the day to stop. First, confess your sins to God. Then, ask him what actions you should take in order to make things right again.

Repentance begins with confession of our guilt and recognition that our sin is against God.

CHARLES STANLEY

Ten thousand confessions, if they do not spring from really contrite hearts, shall only be additions to their guilt.

C. H. SPURGEON

When true repentance comes, God will not hesitate for a moment to forgive, cast the sins in the sea of forgetfulness, and put the child on the road to restoration.

BETH MOORE

For Further Reflection

Deuteronomy 4:30–31; Proverbs 14:9; Luke 5:30–32; 15:7; 1 John 1:8–9

Today's Prayer

When I stray from your commandments, Lord, I must not only confess my sins, I must also turn from them. When I fall short, help me to change. When I reject your Word and your will for my life, guide me back to your side. Forgive my sins, dear Lord, and help me live according to your plan for my life. Your plan is perfect, Father; I am not. Let me trust in you. Amen.

Accepting Life

In their hearts humans plan their course,
but the Lord establishes their steps.

PROVERBS 16:9

If you're like most people, you like being in control. Period. You want things to happen according to your wishes and according to your timetable. But sometimes, God has other plans . . . and he always has the final word.

All of us experience adversity and pain. As human beings with limited comprehension, we can never fully understand the will of our Father in heaven. But as believers in a benevolent God, we must always trust his providence.

When Jesus went to the Mount of Olives, as described in Luke 22, he poured out his heart to God. Jesus knew of the agony that he was destined to endure, but he also knew that God's will must be done. We, like our Savior, face trials that bring fear and trembling to the very depths of our souls, but like Christ, we too must ultimately seek God's will, not our own.

Acceptance means learning to trust God more. Today, think of at least one aspect of your past life that you've been reluctant to accept, and then, prayerfully ask God to help you trust him more by accepting the past.

What cannot be altered must be borne, not blamed.

THOMAS FULLER

Prayer may not get us what we want, but it will teach us to want what we need.

VANCE HAVNER

Trust the past to God's mercy, the present to God's love, and the future to God's providence.

ST. AUGUSTINE

For Further Reflection

Job 2:10; 22:21; Isaiah 43:18–19;
John 18:11; 1 Timothy 4:4

Today's Prayer

Dear Lord, let me live in the present, not the past. Let me focus on my blessings, not my sorrows. Give me the wisdom to be thankful for the gifts that I do have and not bitter about the things that I don't have. Let me accept what was, let me give thanks for what is, and let me have faith in what most surely will be: the promise of eternal life with you. Amen.

Acknowledging God's Presence Builds Character

Come near to God and he will come near to you.

James 4:8

In the quiet early morning, as the sun's first rays peak over the horizon, we may sense the presence of God. But as the day wears on and the demands of everyday life bear down upon us, we may become so wrapped up in earthly concerns that we forget to praise the Creator.

God is everywhere we have ever been and everywhere we will ever be. We are free to sense his presence whenever we take the time to quiet our souls and turn our prayers to him. When we turn to him often, we are blessed by his presence. But if we ignore God's presence or rebel against it altogether, the world in which we live soon becomes a spiritual wasteland.

- Are you tired, discouraged, or fearful? Be comforted because God is with you.
- Are you confused? Listen to the quiet voice of your heavenly Father.
- Are you bitter? Talk with God and seek his guidance.
- Are you celebrating a great victory? Thank God and praise him.

God is the Giver of all things good. In whatever condition you find yourself–whether you are happy or sad, victorious or vanquished, troubled or triumphant–

celebrate God's presence. And be comforted in the knowledge that God is not just near, he is here.

Having trouble hearing God? If so, slow yourself down, tune out the distractions, and listen carefully. God has important things to say; your task is to be still and listen.

There is a basic urge: the longing for unity. You desire a reunion with God–with God your Father.

E. Stanley Jones

The next time your hear a baby laugh or see an ocean wave, take note. Pause and listen as his Majesty whispers ever so gently, "I'm here."

Max Lucado

Get yourself into the presence of the loving Father. Just place yourself before Him, and look up into, His face; think of His love, His wonderful, tender, pitying love.

Andrew Murray

For Further Reflection

2 Chronicles 16:9; Jeremiah 29:13; John 14:18; Acts 17:27; 1 John 3:23-24

Today's Prayer

Dear Lord, you are with me always. Help me feel your presence in every situation and every circumstance. Today, dear God, let me feel you and acknowledge your presence, your love, and your Son. Amen.

Overcoming Addiction Builds Character

Be alert and of sober mind. Your enemy the devil prowls around like a roaring lion looking for someone to devour. Resist him, standing firm in the faith.

1 PETER 5:8–9

Our society glamorizes the use of drugs, alcohol, cigarettes, and other addictive substances. Why? One word: money. Addictive substances are big moneymakers, so suppliers (of both legal and illegal substances) work overtime to create a steady stream of new customers because the old ones are dying off (fast).

The dictionary defines addiction as "the compulsive need for a habit-forming substance; the condition of being habitually and compulsively occupied with something." That definition is accurate but incomplete. For Christians, addiction has an additional meaning: it means compulsively worshiping something other than God.

Unless you're living on a deserted island, you know people who are full-blown addicts—maybe lots of people. If you, or someone you love, is suffering from the blight of addiction, remember this: help is available. Plenty of people have experienced addiction and lived to tell about it, so don't give up hope.

And if you're one of those fortunate people who hasn't started experimenting with addictive substances, congratulations! You have just spared yourself a lifetime of headaches and heartaches.

Remember that ultimately, you and you alone are responsible for controlling your appetites. Others may warn you, help you, or encourage you; but in the end, the habits that rule your life are the very same habits that you yourself have formed. Thankfully, since you formed these habits, you can also break them—and deciding to break them is the first step in doing so.

We are meant to be addicted to God, but we develop secondary addictions that temporarily appear to fix our problem.

Edward M. Berckman

Addiction is the most powerful psychic enemy of humanity's desire for God.

Gerald May

The soul that journeys to God, but doesn't shake off its cares and quiet its appetites, is like someone who drags a cart uphill.

St. John of the Cross

For Further Reflection

Exodus 20:3; Proverbs 5:23; John 8:34; Romans 8:37; Hebrews 4:15–16

Today's Prayer

Dear Lord, you have instructed me to care for my body, and I will obey you. I will be mindful of the destructive power of addiction, and I will avoid the people, the places, and the substances that can entrap my spirit and destroy my life. Amen.

Hard Work Builds Character

Never be lacking in zeal, but keep your spiritual fervor, serving the Lord.

ROMANS 12:11

Whether you're in school or in the workplace, your success will depend, in large part, upon the passion that you bring to your work. God has created a world in which diligence is rewarded and sloth is not. So whatever you choose to do, do it with commitment, with excitement, with enthusiasm, and with vigor.

In his second letter to the Thessalonians, Paul warns, "The one who is unwilling to work shall not eat" (3:10). And the book of Proverbs proclaims, "One who is slack in his work is brother to one who destroys" (18:9). Clearly, God's Word commends the value and importance of diligence. Yet we live in a world that, all too often, glorifies leisure while downplaying the importance of shoulder-to-the-wheel hard work. Rest assured, however, that God does not underestimate the value of diligence. And neither should you.

God did not create you to be ordinary; he created you for far greater things. Reaching for greater things usually requires work and lots of it, which is perfectly fine with God. After all, he knows that you're up to the task, and he has big plans for you. Very big plans.

Here's a time-tested formula for success: have faith in God and do the work. It has been said that there are no shortcuts to any place worth going. Hard work is not simply a proven way to get ahead, but it's also part of God's plan for all his children (including you).

Chiefly the mold of a man's fortune is in his own hands.

FRANCIS BACON

How do I love God? By doing beautifully the work I have been given to do, by doing simply that which God entrusted to me, in whatever form it may take.

MOTHER TERESA

If you want to reach your potential, you need to add a strong work ethic to your talent.

JOHN MAXWELL

For Further Reflection

1 Chronicles 28:20; 2 Chronicles 31:21;
1 Corinthians 3:8; 15:57–58; Colossians 3:23

Today's Prayer

Lord, let me be an industrious worker in your fields. Those fields are ripe, Lord, and your workers are few. Let me be counted as your faithful, diligent servant today and every day. Amen.

Building Character by Finding Courage

Be strong and courageous, and do the work.
Do not be afraid or discouraged, for the
Lord God, my God, is with you.

1 Chronicles 28:20

Courage builds character and vice versa. So if you'd like a brief course in character building, try this: the next time you face a choice between doing the right thing or the easy thing, summon the courage to do the right thing. And while you're summoning that courage, ask God to help.

The following words from Billy Graham apply to you:

> *Down through the centuries, in times of trouble and trial, God has brought courage to the hearts of those who love him. The Bible is filled with assurances of God's help and comfort in every kind of trouble which might cause fears to arise in the human heart. You can look ahead with promise, hope, and joy.*

The next time you find your courage tested by the inevitable challenges of life, remember that God is as near as your next breath. He is your shield and your strength; he is your protector and your deliverer. Call upon him in your hour of need and then be comforted. Whatever your challenge, whatever your trouble, God can handle it. And will.

Is your courage being tested today? Cling tightly to God's promises, and pray. God can give you the strength to meet any challenge, and that's exactly what you should ask him to do.

Take courage. We walk in the wilderness today and in the Promised Land tomorrow.

D. L. Moody

What is courage? It is the ability to be strong in trust, in conviction, in obedience. To be courageous is to step out in faith–to trust and obey, no matter what.

Kay Arthur

Do not let Satan deceive you into being afraid of God's plans for your life.

R. A. Torrey

For Further Reflection

Deuteronomy 31:8; Psalm 71:1; Isaiah 41:10; John 14:27; Philippians 4:13

Today's Prayer

Lord, at times this world is a fearful place. I fear for my family and friends. Yet you have promised me that you are with me always. With you as my protector, I am not afraid. Today, dear Lord, let me live courageously as I place my trust in you. Amen.

Gratitude Builds Character

Give thanks in all circumstances; for this is God's will for you in Christ Jesus.

1 Thessalonians 5:18

As Christians, we are blessed beyond measure. But sometimes, in the crush of everyday living, we simply don't stop long enough to pause and thank our Creator for the countless blessings he has bestowed upon us. Thanksgiving should become a habit, a regular part of our daily routine. God has blessed us beyond measure, and we owe him everything, including our eternal praise.

- Are you a thankful person?
- Do you appreciate the gifts that God has given you?
- Do you demonstrate your gratitude by being a faithful steward of the gifts and talents that you have received from your Creator?

You most certainly should be thankful. After all, when you stop to think about it, God has given you more blessings than you can count. So the question of the day is this: Will you thank your heavenly Father, or will you spend your time and energy doing other things?

God is always listening–are you willing to say thanks? It's up to you, and the next move is yours.

Since you're thankful to God, tell him so. And keep telling him so every day of your life.

We ought to give thanks for all fortune: if it is good, because it is good, if bad, because it works in us patience, humility, and the contempt of this world along with the hope of our eternal country.

C. S. Lewis

A sense of gratitude for God's presence in our lives will help open our eyes to what he has done in the past and what he will do in the future.

Emilie Barnes

When it comes to life, the critical thing is whether you take things for granted or take them with gratitude.

G. K. Chesterton

For Further Reflection

Psalms 92:1; 100:4-5; 2 Corinthians 9:15; Colossians 2:6-7; 3:17

Today's Prayer

Lord, you have blessed me with both family and friends. Make me a person who is thankful, loving, responsible, and wise. I praise you, Father, for the gift of your Son and for the gift of salvation. Let me be a joyful Christian and a worthy example this day and every day that I live. Amen.

The Right Kind of Attitude

All the days of the oppressed are wretched,
but the cheerful heart has a continual feast.

Proverbs 15:15

What's your attitude today?

- Are you fearful, angry, bored, or worried?
- Are you pessimistic, perplexed, pained, or perturbed?
- Are you moping around with a frown on your face that's almost as big as the one in your heart?

If so, God wants to have a little talk with you.

God created you in his own image, and he wants you to experience joy, contentment, peace, and abundance. But you must claim them for yourself. God has given you free will, including the ability to influence the direction and the tone of your thoughts.

Here's how God wants you to direct those thoughts:

> *Finally, brothers and sisters, whatever is true, whatever is noble, whatever is right, whatever is pure, whatever is lovely, whatever is admirable–if anything is excellent or praiseworthy–think about such things* (Philippians 4:8).

So the next time you find yourself dwelling upon the negative aspects of your life, refocus your attention on positive things.

Today, create a positive attitude by focusing on opportunities, not roadblocks. Of course you may have experienced disappointments in the past, and you will undoubtedly experience some setbacks in the future. But don't invest large amounts of energy focusing on past misfortunes. Instead, look to the future with optimism and hope.

The people whom I have seen succeed best in life have always been cheerful and hopeful people who went about their business with a smile on their faces.

CHARLES KINGSLEY

Keep your feet on the ground, but let your heart soar as high as it will. Refuse to be average or to surrender to the chill of your spiritual environment.

A. W. TOZER

Developing a positive attitude means working continually to find what is uplifting and encouraging.

BARBARA JOHNSON

For Further Reflection

2 Corinthians 9:7; Philippians 2:5–8; 4:8; Colossians 3:2; Hebrews 4:12

Today's Prayer

Lord, let me be an expectant Christian. Let me expect the best from you, and let me look for the best in others. If I become discouraged, Father, turn my thoughts and my prayers to you. Let me trust you, Lord, to direct my life. And let me share my faith and optimism with others today and every day that I live. Amen.

A Regular Daily Devotional Builds Character

He wakens me morning by morning, wakens my ear to listen like one being instructed. The Sovereign Lord has opened my ears.

Isaiah 50:4–5

Do you have a character-building, life-altering, standing appointment with God every morning? Is God your first priority, or do talk with him less frequently than that? If you're wise, you'll talk to God first thing every day, without exception.

When you begin each day with your head bowed and your heart lifted, you are reminded of God's love, his protection, and his commandments. Then, you can align your priorities for the coming day with the teachings and commandments that God has placed upon your heart.

If you've acquired the unfortunate habit of trying to squeeze God into the corners of your life, it's time to reshuffle the items on your to-do list by placing God first. And if you haven't already done so, form the habit of spending quality time each morning with your Creator. He deserves it . . . and so, for that matter, do you.

Get reacquainted with God every day. Would you like a foolproof formula for a better life? Here it is: stay in close contact with God.

We must appropriate the tender mercy of God every day after conversion or problems quickly develop. We need his grace daily in order to live a righteous life.

Jim Cymbala

I suggest you discipline yourself to spend time daily in a systematic reading of God's Word. Make this "quiet time" a priority that nobody can change.

Warren Wiersbe

God is a place of safety you can run to, but it helps if you are running to Him on a daily basis so that you are in familiar territory.

Stormie Omartian

For Further Reflection

Psalms 46:10; 63:1; Matthew 6:33;
Mark 1:35-36; James 4:8

Today's Prayer

Lord, help me to hear your direction for my life in the quiet moments when I study your Holy Word. And as I go about my daily activities, let everything that I say and do be pleasing to you. Amen.

For God So Loved the World

God so loved the world that he gave his one and only Son, that whoever believes in him shall not perish but have eternal life.

John 3:16

God's grace is not earned . . . thank goodness! To earn God's love and his gift of eternal life would be far beyond the abilities of even the most righteous man or woman. Thankfully, grace is not an earthly reward for righteous behavior; it is a blessed spiritual gift that can be accepted by believers who dedicate themselves to God through Christ. When we accept Christ into our hearts, we are saved by his grace.

God's grace is the ultimate gift, and we owe to him the ultimate in thanksgiving. Let us praise the Creator for his priceless gift, and let us share the Good News with all who cross our paths. We return our Father's love by accepting his grace and by sharing his message and his love. When we do, we are eternally blessed . . . and the hosts of heaven rejoice!

The time is now. If you have already welcomed Christ into your heart as your personal savior, then you are safe. If you're still sitting on the fence, the time to accept him is this very moment.

God did everything necessary to provide for our forgiveness by sacrificing His perfect, holy Son as the atoning substitute for our sins.

FRANKLIN GRAHAM

The way to be saved is not to delay, but to come and take.

D. L. MOODY

We had better quickly discover whether we have mere religion or a real experience with Jesus, whether we have outward observance of religious forms or hearts that beat in tune with God.

JIM CYMBALA

For Further Reflection

Acts 2:20–21; 4:10, 12; 1 Timothy 1:15; 1 Peter 1:3; 1 John 4:14

Today's Prayer

Dear Lord, I am only here on this earth for a brief while. But you have offered me the priceless gift of eternal life through your Son, Jesus. I accept your gift, Lord, with thanksgiving and praise. Let me share the Good News of my salvation with all those who need your healing touch. Amen.

ISBN:9781628624953